ASMA'S
INDIAN·KITCHEN

ASMA'S
INDIAN·KITCHEN

Asma Khan

PAVILION

First published in the United Kingdom in 2018 by
Pavilion
43 Great Ormond Street
London
WC1N 3HZ

ISBN: 978-1-911595-68-7

A CIP catalogue record for this book is available from the British Library.

10 9 8 7 6 5 4

Reproduction by Mission, Hong Kong
Printed and bound by 1010 Printing International Ltd, China

www.pavilionbooks.com

_____

Note to readers: Both metric and imperial measurements (plus US cups)
appear within these recipes, however it is important to work with one set of
measurements and not alternate between the two within a recipe. The oven
temperatures listed are for conventional ovens. If using a fan oven, reduce
the heat by 20°C. Be aware that oven temperatures vary between appliances
and adjust if necessary.

My Indian Kitchen

An immigrant's food story

When I arrived in the UK from Calcutta to join my husband, I could not cook anything. I would buy discounted Indian cookbooks from bookshops in Cambridge to gaze at the photographs, which would remind me of the familiar flavours of home. During my first winter in England, the River Cam froze over. I remember the cold, damp wind slicing into me as I practised how to cycle on Parker's Piece. I felt sure everyone had got the description of hell wrong: it was not fire that awaited you, it was frozen rivers, icy winds, and a kitchen that was infused with none of the aromas of home.

During one of my practice cycle sessions, I ventured a bit further than usual and wheeled past a house where inside someone was making parathas. I jumped off my bicycle. From outside where I stood, I could smell the bread frying in ghee. I wanted so desperately to ring the doorbell and ask if the person making the paratha might share it with me. But I did not walk up to that door. Instead, I stood rooted to the pavement and cried.

In that moment, I realized the only way I could make this unfamiliar place feel like home was to cook the food of my home. This is how my food journey began. I set about cooking so that my one-room apartment in Cambridge might start to feel more of a home. The house I was living in was a college residence, but rather than digs for students, it was home to fellows teaching at the university. I was neither a fellow nor a student and did not know anyone in the college. I needed to make friends in the city and I thought that if I cooked, I could invite guests to the flat, share a meal and maybe find a way to connect with them through food.

Over the years, I have discovered that food is a wonderful unifying force, providing a way for immigrants to make connections in a new country. Breaking bread with others leads to conversations about 'home', no matter how far away that place might be or how little knowledge of a country or culture people may have. I am always willing to share a plate of parathas with those who knock at my door.

My family food heritage

I am fortunate to have inherited the culinary heritage of both my paternal and maternal royal traditions. On my paternal side, I am a descendant from the ancient Rajput Suryavanshi warrior Bargujar clan. During the reign of the third Mughal ruler, my ancestor Lal Singh was given the title of Lal Khan by the Mughal Emperor Akbar for his bravery. Our family are called Lalkhani Rajputs after Lal Khan. My paternal family converted to Islam in the reign of Emperor Akbar's son and settled in Bulandshahr. They adopted the food tradition of the Mughal courts, while their geographical proximity to Lucknow meant that rare and exotic spices from Turkey and Persia were available more easily.

My maternal family was from North Bengal. My ancestor Khan Bahadur Musharraf Husain, the Nawab of Jalpaiguri, was a pioneering tea planter instrumental in establishing new tea plantations in Darjeeling with seeds he had acquired from China. By the time of his death, my maternal family owned 33 tea gardens in the Darjeeling area. In the 1940s, my maternal family moved from Jalpaiguri and Darjeeling to live in Calcutta. Their ceremonial feasting foods were distinctive Calcutta Mughlai dishes, including Mutton Dum Biryani, Mutton Rezala and Calcutta Chicken Chaap.

Two of the other food influences on my life are reflected in this book. The first is the Bihari Muslim food from the home of my maternal grandmother, who came from the principality of Bakhtiyarpur. The halwas and desserts of the palace were very unusual: kheer is a rice and milk pudding, which the cooks supposedly made using onions! (For my version of Boora Chenni Ki Kheer, see page 96.) The kitchens in Bakhtiyarpur are still run by the same family of cooks who cooked during my great-great-grandmother's time. The egg dish, Unday Ka Halwa (see page 95), is a wonderful recipe and comes from this branch of my family.

My family has also enjoyed a long and close relationship with the royal family of Hyderabad. During the 1940s, my paternal great-grandfather was the Prime Minister of the Nizam State and was involved in the negotiations between the British and Indian politicians that eventually led to the royal state of Hyderabad joining the Indian Republic. I lived in Hyderabad as a child. It is of this city that I have my earliest memories: attending spectacular feasts in beautiful old homes where many of the dishes served were too spicy for me to enjoy as a child. The food left a deep impression on me. Amongst my favourite recipes are unique Hyderabadi dishes, such as Haleem, Baghare Baigan, Tamatar Ka Cutt, Mirchi Ka Salaan and Khoobani Ka Meetha to mention a few.

While the Hyderabadi recipes are a distinctive mix of South Indian spices and North Indian cooking traditions, some dishes are surprisingly easy to make. This book includes the recipe for the Hyderabadi side dish, Tamatar Ka Cutt (hard-boiled eggs in a slow-cooked tomato sauce, see page 80), which can transform a simple meal into something extraordinary.

Many of the royal recipes and cooking traditions from both my father's and mother's sides of the family have been passed on to me. It is these wonderful dishes, with their rich heritage and spice traditions, which I would like to share with you in this book. And it was these dishes that I started to cook after arriving in the UK from India; over the years I have learnt to recreate my traditional family recipes in my modest Cambridge and London kitchens. These dishes are impressive enough to become the centrepiece of a large gathering of family or friends, but are also simple enough to be recreated in any home kitchen.

Feasts

Food is at the heart of every Indian celebration. There is nothing more joyous than bringing loved ones together around a table and sharing a meal. Whether that is a weekday supper for two or a lavish celebration spread, there is no reason why each and every meal should not be a feast fit for royalty.

This book has been divided by occasions, from a feast for two to a large gathering of family and friends. The recipes in the Feasts for Two chapter are not just for when you are planning an intimate dinner with a loved one, they are also to cook when you want to spoil yourself after a gruelling day. I find cooking very cathartic. When not everything has gone to plan during the day, you can re-take control in the evening and cook a special, nurturing meal for yourself – something that always makes me feel better.

The Family Feasts chapter contains many of my favourite crowd-pleasing recipes that will win over even the most spice-sensitive, picky eaters. The level of spice and heat can be easily adjusted in these dishes, depending on whether you are catering for children as well as adults, or even adults who prefer their dishes on the milder side.

When entertaining friends at home, I don't want to spend all my time in the kitchen rather than relaxing with my guests. With this in mind, the Feasting with Friends recipes have all been selected to give you enough time to cook and clear away, ensuring that you do not end up stood over the stove at the very last minute.

Finally, I hope the recipes in the Celebratory Feasts chapter will inspire you to be a little more adventurous than you may have been before when cooking Indian food. Some of these recipes do involve a reasonable amount of preparation and cooking time, but the results are truly show-stopping centrepiece dishes that befit their royal heritage.

Breaking bread and sharing food with people you care for should be a happy, joyous occasion. You can be the bridge, bringing together people from all sides around your table. Food is pleasure. I hope cooking, eating and sharing the recipes from this book will give you as much pleasure as it gave me writing it.

Techniques to elevate your Indian cooking

Back home in Calcutta, an exceptional family cook was a prized asset. We inherited our cook, Haji Saheb, from my mother's great grand aunt, Choti Dadu, who passed him to our family as the greatest gift she could have endowed upon us after her death. In a society where access to the same ingredients meant that everyone could cook identical dishes, what elevated one family's food above another's was the subtlety with which the ingredients were handled. It was a delicacy of touch that was most highly regarded when it came to cooking. I encourage you to handle your ingredients with the same lightness of touch. When it comes to adding spices and seasoning to a dish, remember that it is far easier to add than it is to take away. Do take a moment to read through the techniques I describe over the following pages. When followed, they will not only improve the finished dish when cooking the recipes in this book but they will also add depth and flavour to any other Indian recipe you might cook from other cookbooks.

Cooking with onions

There is no shortcut when it comes to browning onions. The first step is to peel the onion and cut it in half around the middle. After that, thinly slice each onion half into neat rings. Try to cut the rings as thinly and as evenly as possible. In order for the onion rings to cook evenly in the hot oil, it is more important that the rings are cut evenly, so aim for a thickness that you know you can cut consistently across the entire onion.

Next, heat the oil over a medium–high heat in a heavy-based frying pan (skillet). Pick up one onion ring and dip the edge into the hot oil, keeping your fingers at a safe distance from the oil's surface. The onion should immediately start to sizzle. If that does not happen, your oil is not hot enough, so wait a further 5 minutes and test again. Once the onion ring sizzles on contact with the hot oil, you are ready to fry the onions. When you are ready to cook the onions, place a slotted spoon and a large plate next to the stove.

Carefully lower all of the onion rings into the hot oil. The temperature of the oil will drop once the onions are in the pan, but it will soon go back up and the onions will start to sizzle. Stir the onions gently around the pan. Initially the oil will turn cloudy as the onions start to release their water into the oil. After 10 minutes or so, that cloudiness will have gone and the onions will now look glossy, and possibly slightly pink. At this point, sprinkle a large pinch of salt over the onions. This was something I learnt from our family cook: the salt drains the water from the onions and speeds up the browning process. I say 'speeds up'; browning onions is a slow process and they will need at least another 20 minutes in the pan.

Throughout the cooking time, keep stirring the onions to ensure they cook evenly and eventually their edges will turn golden brown and they will become a lovely caramel shade in the middle. As well as seeing the onions turn a rich brown colour, you will be able to smell when they are ready. Your kitchen, your clothes, your hair, even your neighbour's flat will smell of luscious caramelized onions!

Remember I said to place a slotted spoon and a large plate next to the frying onions? As soon as the onions are caramelized, it is important to remove them from the oil rapidly and safely. I have burnt many batches of onions while desperately searching to find the right spoon and plate. Using the slotted spoon, scoop the onions from the hot oil and transfer them to the large plate. Then spread the onions out across the plate and, using a fork, separate any onion rings that have stuck to each other. Leave the onions on the plate to cool and crisp up. I find placing the onions on a plate, rather than on paper towels, gives the best, most crispy caramelized onions.

Perfecting the art of caramelizing onions is an important skill for all Indian cooking; beautifully browned and crisped onions will make an enormous difference to every dish you cook. The colour, the aroma, and the flavour of slow-cooked caramelized crispy onions are simply wonderful.

Cooking with chillis

When cooking with chillis, I prefer to embrace the flavour of the chilli in a dish rather than its fiery heat. Often, I leave the chillis whole so they can easily be removed before serving. If you have the time and the patience, then you may want to employ a technique taught to me by our family cook. He would make very tiny incisions along the sides of the green chillis to increase the chilli flavour in a dish without letting loose all the scorching heat from the seeds and membranes inside the chillis. If the chillis you are using are mild, you could slice them in half.

Where a dish calls for sliced or chopped chillis, it is considerate towards your guests to chop the chillis into pieces that are large enough for them to see. That way, anyone who wants to avoid the flaming punch of the chilli can avoid eating them, whilst those who love their intense heat can eat as many as they care to.

You may notice I use a lot of dried red chillies in my recipes, rather than red chilli powder. Infusing chilli flavour by using a whole or broken-in-half dried red chilli gives a dish a more subtle and layered flavour. Chilli powder can often burn the mouth when eaten in a dish; dried red chillis are kinder to the mouth as their flavour is infused in the other ingredients and is not the first thing that hits your tastebuds. The flavour from the dried red chilli does kick in, just not at the very beginning.

I have noticed friends with sensitive stomachs, who have struggled to eat very spicy Indian food, have no problems eating my food. This is possibly because their stomachs do not need to digest chilli powder. I have no scientific proof for that theory, it is simply an observation I have made over years of cooking!

Cooking with spices

The pure essence of a spice is contained within the oils trapped inside the spice seed. Gently roasting the spices in a dry pan over a low heat releases those oils. This is a vital stage in all Indian cooking. When liquid is then added to the cooking pot with the dry roasted spices, the oils within the spices slowly infuse the cooking liquid, seeping into the dish and adding subtle layers of flavour.

Spices can quickly burn and easily become bitter, so when dry roasting it is important keep the heat low and constantly turn the spice seeds in the pan using a spoon so that the seeds roast evenly. The aim of roasting spices is to get the heat all the way to the core of the seeds and release the aromas. A spice seed darkens as it roasts, but the change in colour can be very subtle and made harder when a spice is already dark in colour, such as cumin. I recommend keeping a small bowl of unroasted seeds close to the pan in which you are roasting the spices – that way you can compare the roasted and unroasted seeds and note any differences in colour. As soon as the spices have darkened, tip them on to a plate to prevent them cooking further in the hot pan. Once the spices are cool, you can grind them to a powder using a spice grinder or a pestle and mortar.

If you over-roast any spices, always throw them away and start again. There is nothing more unpleasant than the bitter undertone of a burnt spice in a dish.

Cassia bark and cinnamon sticks
Compared to the lighter, orange-brown curled cinnamon stick, cassia bark is a darker, flatter, more obviously bark-like stick. Frequently, both cinnamon and cassia bark are labelled (incorrectly) as cinnamon. For me, the delicate edge of cinnamon makes it perfect for sweet dishes, whilst cassia bark has a more robust flavour that takes heat far better than cinnamon. I have suggested cassia bark for all the meat and rice recipes in this book, but if you only have cinnamon then of course you can use that instead.

Indian bay leaves
Another confusion often occurs between the leaf of the European Bay Laurel tree, which is dark green in colour and most commonly used in Mediterranean cooking, and the Indian bay leaf, which is larger and olive green in colour. Indian bay leaves are called Tej Patta, which means 'pungent leaf'. The flavour released by the Indian bay leaf during cooking is totally different from the European bay leaf. Often Tej Pattas are labelled as 'bay leaves' so look at the size and colour of the leaves to pick the right one! Tej Pattas release a strong, robust cassia-bark-style flavour when cooked, while bay laurel leaves impart a more Mediterranean flavour of lemons and pine nuts.

Turmeric
Raw ground turmeric can be quite unpleasant, however it only takes a few seconds of cooking to get rid of its raw smell. In a hot pan, stir the turmeric for 10–20 seconds or until the smell disappears. It does only take another few extra seconds in the pan to burn, so watch ground turmeric carefully and do not let the spice burn.

Garam masala

Garam masala is a mix of spices used in large areas of the Indian subcontinent. Garam means 'heat': according to Ayurveda, many of the spices included in garam masala, like cinnamon and cloves, raise the body temperature. The flavour gained from home-made garam masala is a world apart from anything you can buy in a packet from a store. Sometimes the garam masalas are used whole, as in the recipes for Murgh Rezala (see page 66), whilst at other times the spices are ground and used as a powder. Grinding small batches of dry roasted spices, which can then be kept in an airtight container, will greatly enhance any dish you cook that calls for garam masala.

The recipe for my garam masala blend is below. I add both nutmeg and mace to my mix, two distinctly flavoured spices from the same fragrant tree. Mace is the outside covering of the nutmeg seed, with a more delicate flavour than the nutmeg seed. Also, I prefer to use cassia bark, rather than cinnamon sticks. However, making garam masala is not an exact science. If you find you are short of one spice, it isn't a huge problem. To help you locate spices in a store or order them online, I have listed the Indian terms first, as many packets have the Indian name written more prominently than the English.

Dalchini/cassia bark (often labelled as cinnamon)	1 piece, 5 cm/2 inches long
Laung/cloves	8
Bari kali elaichee/black cardamom (optional)	4
Choti hari elaichee/green cardamom	12
Kali mirch/black peppercorns	1 tsp
Jaiphal/nutmeg (freshly grated)	¼ tsp
Jaivitri/mace (crushed)	¼ tsp
Tej patta/Indian bay leaves	2 large leaves

Warm a heavy-based frying pan (skillet) over a low–medium heat. If you have a tawa or cast-iron griddle pan, use that as the heat is more evenly distributed. Place a plate next to the pan, ready to transfer the roasted spices. Do not use paper towels as they will soak up the precious oils released by heating the spices. Heat each of the spices individually in the warm pan. (The Tej patta or Indian bay leaves do not necessarily need to be heated, see below.) The time this takes depends on the heat of the pan and size of the spices. Aim to warm the spices evenly, so keep turning them using a spoon.

When roasted, cassia bark darkens a couple of shades. Place an unroasted piece of cassia bark next to the pan so you can make a visual comparison with the bark you are roasting and gauge how much it has darkened. Cloves are easy to roast, as you can see their transformation. The base of the clove expands and brown patches appear. The moment that happens, take the cloves off the heat and spread out on the plate. Both the cardamom and the peppercorns can be roasted for 15–20 seconds before tipping onto the plate. The nutmeg and mace should be in the hot pan for only a few seconds.

Once cool, all the garam masala spices can be ground to a fine powder either in a spice grinder or with a pestle and mortar. If you are using a pestle and mortar, heat the Indian bay leaves in the pan for a few seconds to make them brittle and then crush them by hand before adding to the spices in the mortar. If using a spice grinder, break the Indian bay leaves into pieces and add them to the spices. Store in an airtight container.

Panchporan

Very few recipes call for the five-seed spice blend known as panchporan. As you probably won't use up a home-made panchporan mix that quickly, a better option is to buy a small quantity of a ready-made blend rather than buy quantities of each individual spice seed. Panchporan is almost always used whole.

Char magaz

The literal translation of char magaz is 'four brains'. The ingredients that make up char magaz are packed with nutrients, which some people consider to have brain-boosting properties! Char magaz can be purchased ready packaged in Indian grocery stores and from online retailers, or you can make the mix yourself. The combination our family cook would use was musk melon seeds, watermelon seeds, pumpkin seeds and almonds. If you don't have char magaz to hand, you can substitute finely ground almonds or pine nuts.

A note on seasoning

The amount of salt needed in a dish depends on your preference, so always taste to check the seasoning and adjust by adding a pinch more salt or sugar as necessary. Add just a small amount of salt initially and then taste and adjust throughout the cooking process. If you do happen to add too much salt to any dish, adding pieces of potato can help to ameliorate the effects as it will absorb some of the excess salt. Peel a large potato and cut it into quarters lengthwise. Add these potato pieces the pan and leave them in there for at least 15 minutes whilst the dish cooks. Using a slotted spoon, scoop out the potato pieces and either discard them or use them in another potato dish.

Feasts for Two

Food for the soul

As a cook, you are the vehicle to heal and nourish the soul. Your food should feel like an embrace. This is my mother's food philosophy. As one of five daughters, my mother is the only one who is an accomplished cook. At any family gathering or occasion, the responsibility to decide on a menu that will please everyone, then arrange and order the food, always falls to my mother. She seems to thrive in that role, taking pride in making sure all her guests are content during a meal.

It was only once I started cooking and serving my food to others that I fully understood this philosophy. I began hosting my first dawaats, or feasts, as a student in Cambridge. Most of the guests were South Asian in origin and the first thing I noticed was the silence that descended when the guests started eating – as if everything stopped for that moment. I knew then what my mother meant when she said one should cook to nourish the soul. I felt it in that moment of silence. My guests had been transported back home, back to another world, miles away from the spires of the university town of Cambridge. Food has the ability to carry you away to another moment and place, the aromas and flavours reminding you of a time when you ate something similar. With many of our guests at my restaurant Darjeeling Express, I witness that moment when they are eating – that silent moment – and I know that I have fed their souls.

Aloo Bharta
Spicy potato mash <u>v</u>

Bengal is the land of bhortas – the Bengali pronunciation of the Hindi word 'bharta', which means mashed. There are many variations on this dish. Here I am giving the recipe for two of my favourite versions. One is a mix of fresh, raw ingredients while the other requires a bit of cooking. Either way, Aloo Bharta goes perfectly with dal and rice. If you want to make this dish for more than two people, multiply the quantities given below.

Serves 2

2 large baking potatoes (approximately 500 g/1 lb 2 oz)

For the fresh, raw version

2 tbsp mustard oil, olive oil or argan oil

½ tsp salt

1 green chilli, finely chopped

1 small shallot or red onion, finely chopped

1 tbsp finely chopped coriander (cilantro) leaves

For the cooked version

2 tbsp mustard oil, olive oil or argan oil

½ tsp salt

1 dried red chilli, broken into small pieces

2 garlic cloves, thinly sliced

1 small shallot or red onion, finely chopped

Small handful of coriander (cilantro) leaves, to garnish

Cook the potatoes by either baking or boiling them using your preferred method. While the potatoes are still warm but cool enough to handle, remove their skins. In a bowl, mash the potatoes until smooth, using a masher or fork.

To make the fresh, raw version, simply add all the other ingredients to the mashed potato and mix. Serve at room temperature.

To make the cooked version, in a frying pan (skillet), heat the oil, add all the other ingredients, except the coriander leaves, and fry until brown. Add the warm fried onion mixture to the mashed potatoes and mix. Serve at room temperature with a few fresh coriander leaves scattered over the top.

Zeera Aloo
Potatoes with cumin V

A quick and simple potato dish, which goes well with bread or rice. The quantities given here make generous helpings for two. If you are serving a lot of other dishes, you may want to halve the amounts. Alternatively, if you decide to make this for more than two people, simply double, treble or quadruple the quantities of each ingredient. Personally, I think you can never make too many potatoes. Use the widest pan that you have to cook this dish – ideally one in which the potato slices do not overlap.

Serves 2

2 large potatoes (standard white potatoes, such as Maris Piper, approximately 500 g/ 1 lb 2 oz), cut in half and thinly sliced

4 tbsp vegetable oil

1 tsp cumin seeds

4 dried red chillis

¾ tsp salt

In a bowl, soak the potato slices in cold water for 10 minutes, then rinse under cold running water to remove any excess starch. Dry the potatoes on paper towels.

In a wide saucepan, heat the oil over a medium–high heat. Add the cumin seeds to the pan followed by the dried red chillis, then cook, stirring, for a few seconds until the cumin seeds and chillis darken and release their aromas. (If you enjoy the flavour of chilli but not the heat, use the dried red chillis whole. However, if you like the heat, break the chillis in half before adding to the pan so they release more of their fiery heat into the dish.)

Add the potato slices to the pan in a single layer, trying not to overlap them, then add the salt. Allow the oil to return to a medium heat before lowering. Gently cook over a low heat until the potatoes take on a translucent glaze and break easily. To prevent the potatoes from breaking up during cooking, do not stir too often – the best way to ensure even cooking is to shake the pan and then carefully turn the potatoes.

Standard white potatoes work best for this dish, rather than floury potatoes that will fall apart while cooking.

Courgette Sabzi <u>V</u>

This simple Bengali dish is usually made from leftover vegetables – whatever you have to hand that are ripe and big enough to cut up. In my home we often used young turai, a local Indian vegetable that is similar to courgette, but beans and carrots both work well cooked in this way because they are relatively quick to cook. In fact, because Indians are very frugal and don't throw anything away, I've often seen this dish made with the vegetable peelings. It's a great way to use up veggies and, equally, it makes what you have got a bit further.

I've used courgette here, which is not a vegetable commonly found in India, but it is available in abundance in other parts of the world. I love its colour and crunchy texture. Courgette Sabzi is very simple to make; you can easily chat to your dinner guest whilst chopping the veg, there is no frying of onions or garlic here – two things that prolong the cooking of Indian food – plus it doesn't generate much mess.

With the dried chillis, nigella seeds and turmeric, it looks and tastes great. Plus it goes with almost everything: meat, fish, I even like it as a filling in Indian bread. Courgette Sabzi is also delicious cold, although less crunchy. Any leftovers are perfect for chucking into your lunch box the next day.

Serves 2 as a main course or 4 as an accompaniment

2 tbsp vegetable oil

2 dried red chillis, broken in half

½ tsp nigella (black onion) seeds

400 g/14 oz courgettes (zucchini) cut into 1-cm/½-inch cubes

½ tsp ground turmeric

½ tsp salt

In a deep pan or wok, heat the oil over a medium–high heat. Add the dried red chillis and nigella seeds to the pan. Immediately add the diced courgette to the pan and stir.

Add the ground turmeric and salt to the pan and then cook, stirring, over a high heat for 2–3 minutes. It is important not to overcook the courgettes: they should still be crunchy and have a little 'bite' to them. The best way to check is to taste a piece: the courgette should be cooked all the way through, but not even close to becoming soft and woolly. Take the pan off the heat while the courgettes are still glossy and firm as they will continue to cook due to the residual heat from the pan.

Before serving, taste to check the seasoning and adjust as necessary.

Tehri
Vegetable pulao V

A meal on its own, Tehri is perfect served simply with yogurt or raita on the side or a crisp Kachumber (see page 166) or crunchy mixed salad. You can replace the diced carrots with any of your favourite vegetables, such as peas, sweetcorn, chopped beans, or a mixture of all if you fancy. This recipe makes a generous amount for two. If there are any leftovers, allow them to cool within an hour of cooking, store in the refrigerator and then reheat thoroughly in a low oven.

Serves 2

225 g/8 oz/1¼ cup basmati rice

2 tbsp vegetable oil

1 piece cassia bark, 2 cm/¾ inches long (see page 13)

2 green cardamom pods

1 small white onion (approximately 50 g/1¾ oz), finely chopped

½ tsp garlic paste

½ tsp fresh ginger paste

½ tsp ground turmeric

¼ tsp chilli powder (adjust to taste)

75 g/2½ oz potatoes, peeled and cut into 1-cm/½-inch cubes

50 g/1¾ oz carrots peeled and cut into 1-cm/½-inch cubes

½ tsp salt (adjust to taste)

Fresh green chillis, sliced, to garnish (optional)

Wash the rice in several changes of cold running water until it runs clear, then place in a bowl and soak for 30 minutes in fresh cold water.

In a heavy-based pan that has a lid, heat the oil over a medium–high heat. Add the cassia bark and cardamom pods to the oil, then stir for a few seconds. Add the onion and cook, stirring, until it starts to colour. Continue stirring to prevent the onions sticking to the base of the pan.

Once the onions have started to brown, add the garlic and ginger pastes. After 1 minute, add the ground turmeric and chilli powder. Cook, stirring, for 10–20 seconds or until the 'raw' smell of the turmeric has disappeared, taking care not to let the ground spices burn.

Add the potatoes and carrots, plus any other vegetables. The water content in the vegetables should add sufficient moisture, but if the mixture sticks to the pan, add a splash of water. Cook the potatoes and vegetables, stirring, for at least 5 minutes to seal them in the oil to prevent them disintegrating when cooked with the rice. The vegetables should be glistening and the potatoes starting to catch along their edges.

Put the kettle on to boil. Add the soaked rice and salt to the pan. Stir for 1 minute to coat the rice in the spices, then cover with 900 ml/30 fl oz/ 3¾ cups boiling water from the kettle. Cook uncovered over a medium–high heat until the water has been almost absorbed (about 4 minutes).

Cover the pan with the lid, lower the heat and simmer for a further 15–20 minutes. Resist the temptation to open the lid. If you do, the trapped steam and aromas will be lost. After 20 minutes, check the rice – there should be no liquid at the edges of the pan – and gently run a fork through to lift and separate the grains. Replace the lid, remove from the heat and leave for a further 5 minutes to allow any remaining moisture to be absorbed. To serve, garnish with sliced fresh green chillis.

Tengri Kabab
Chicken drumstick kabab

When I was growing up in India during the 1970s and 80s, Tengri Kababs were served solely at large family gatherings. As chicken was available whole, the bird was skinned and cut into eight; the drumsticks – tengri means 'leg' – were used to make this dish, while the rest of the meat went into other dishes. With supermarkets opening in India, things are beginning to change and rather than a whole bird, you can now buy chicken in portions, and even a pack of just drumsticks. When cooking this recipe, the Goldilocks Rule applies. You want the drumsticks to be neither too fat, nor too thin. Ideally, they should all be medium so they cooking through evenly without drying out.

Serves 2

4 medium skinless drumsticks (approximately 500 g/1 lb 2 oz)

For the marinade

2 tbsp light soy sauce

1 tbsp lemon juice

½ tbsp ground coriander

¼ tsp chilli powder (replace with paprika for a milder heat)

A large pinch of sugar

1 tbsp fresh ginger paste

1 tbsp garlic paste

Lemon wedges, to serve

In a small bowl, combine all the ingredients for the marinade. Place the chicken drumsticks in a non-reactive container with a lid and pour over the marinade, making sure that every surface of the chicken is covered. Cover the container and place in the refrigerator for a minimum of 6 hours, but preferably overnight.

Take the chicken out of the refrigerator 30 minutes before cooking to allow it to come to room temperature. These kababs can be cooked either in an oven or on a barbecue.

If cooking in an oven, preheat the oven to 200°C/400°F/Gas Mark 6. Place the drumsticks in an oven tray in a single layer to allow then to cook evenly and pour over any remaining marinade. Bake in the oven. After 20–25 minutes, using a sharp knife or skewer, pierce the thickest part of the drumstick to check whether the juices run clear. If not, return to the oven. When cooked, the drumsticks should be speckled with brown patches but the meat should not be dry.

If cooking on a barbecue, wait until any flames have subsided and a low heat is evenly spread across the coals. If the heat is too high, the outsides of the drumsticks will cook quickly but the insides will still be raw. The cooking time will vary depending on the heat of the coals. Before serving, using a sharp knife or skewer, pierce the thickest part of the drumstick to check whether the juices run clear.

Serve the kababs while warm, with lemon wedges to squeeze over.

Chingri Bhaaja
Ghee-fried prawns

Back home in Calcutta, Chingri Bhaaja was made for the most special events when my family had to put on an impressive feast – like a first visit by potential in-laws of one of the cousins! Unlike other prawn dishes, where the size of the prawns used does not necessarily matter, in Chingri Bhaaja, with no gravy to conceal the prawns, they need to be very large indeed in order to impress. As jumbo-sized prawns are more expensive, this is most definitely a special-occasion-only dish.

Serves 2

250 g/9 oz raw tiger prawns (jumbo shrimp), heads removed and deveined

A large pinch of ground turmeric

½ tsp salt (adjust to taste)

2 tbsp ghee

1 small onion, crushed to a paste

2 garlic cloves, crushed to a paste

1 piece fresh ginger, 5 mm/¼ inch long, crushed to a paste

2 dried red chillis

Place the prawns in a bowl, sprinkle over a small pinch of ground turmeric and a large pinch of salt, then leave for 5 minutes.

In a frying pan (skillet) or wok, melt the ghee over a high heat. Add the prawns to the pan and flash-fry for just a few seconds: the prawns should only briefly touch the surface of the pan to seal them, rather than be cooked through. Using a slotted spoon, remove the prawns from the pan, place on a plate and set aside.

To the same pan, add the dried red chillis followed by the onion, garlic and ginger paste and another small pinch of ground turmeric. Fry over a medium–high heat for 5 minutes, or until the 'raw' smell of the paste and turmeric has disappeared. If the paste sticks to the base of the pan, sprinkle over some water.

Return the prawns briefly to the pan and cook, stirring, until the prawns are coated in the cooked paste. The ability to cook prawns perfectly comes with experience. Overcooking makes prawns tough, so keep a close eye on them during frying and cook for no longer than 10 minutes. Taste to check the seasoning and adjust as necessary.

Paneer

Home-made Indian cheese <u>v</u>

When I moved to the UK in 1991, paneer was not available even in small Indian grocery stores. By reading cookbooks in the public library, and combining elements from several different recipes, I learnt to make my own. The quality of milk used to make paneer is paramount. Use the creamiest milk you can find. Rich Jersey cow's milk or buffalo milk are both great for making paneer, but if you cannot source either of those then use homogenized whole milk. Do not attempt to use skimmed or semi-skimmed milk – it is a waste of time and effort.

Makes 500 g (1 lb 2 oz)

4 litres/7 pints/1 gallon plus 1 cup whole milk
120 ml/8 tbsp fresh lemon juice, strained
250 ml/8½ fl oz/1 cup hot water (optional)

Using the right pan to boil the milk is important. One with a thick, heavy base is ideal as the milk must be boiled for a while and should not stick.

Pour the milk into a large heavy-based pan and place over a high heat until the milk comes to a rolling boil. Once the milk is boiling, reduce the heat and allow the bubbles to subside. Stirring gently in a clockwise circular motion, pour the lemon juice into the milk. After stirring for a few moments, take the pan off the heat. Continue to stir in the same direction. Within 1 minute the milk will separate and clumps of curd will form. If nothing happens, do not panic. Put the pan back over a low heat and stir. If nothing happens after another minute, add a further 2 tbsp lemon juice and continue to stir. By now, curds should have formed. Once the curds have formed, leave the pan undisturbed for 10 minutes.

For very soft cheese, gently pour in the hot water from the side. Do not pour the water on top of the curds. As they form, the curds sink to the bottom of the pan. Once the curds have sunk, leaving only the whey at the top of the pan, the curds are ready to drain.

Line a colander with muslin, cheesecloth or Indian malmal (cotton) and place it over a bowl. Using a slotted spoon, scoop all the delicate curds out of the pan and place in the cloth-lined colander to drain. Discard the whey.

Lift the corners of the cloth and tie into a parcel around the curds. Place a heavy pan or other weight on top of the parcel to press any more whey from the curds. After 45 minutes, prod the cheese to check the texture, which should be soft and similar in feel to feta.

Once ready, unwrap the paneer from the cloth and, using paper towels, dab any moisture from the surface of the cheese. The paneer is ready to use straight away or store it in the refrigerator for up to 1 week.

Karai Paneer
Stir-fried Indian cheese V

Due to the time it takes to make paneer, any recipe using this cheese was always considered a 'luxury' vegetarian dish. While home-made paneer (see opposite) gives a superior result, if you don't have the time to make your own, it is widely available in supermarkets. Karai Paneer was the most extravagant of the paneer dishes made in my house as it calls for more of the cheese per head than the more commonly made Saag Paneer (see page 34) or Mattar Paneer (see page 85) where spinach or peas bulk out the dish. Any leftover Karai Paneer can be made into a toasted sandwich, placed between two slices of white bread and fried until golden.

Serves 2

5 tbsp vegetable oil

1 large onion, thinly sliced

1 medium bell pepper, cut into 2-cm/
   ¾-inch cubes

1 small tomato, cut into 2-cm/¾-inch cubes

1 tbsp fresh ginger paste

½ tbsp garlic paste

½ tsp chilli powder

¼ tsp ground turmeric

1 tsp ground coriander

¾ tsp salt

100 ml/3½ fl oz/scant ½ cup full-fat natural
   (plain) yogurt

450–500 g/1 lb–1 lb 2 oz paneer, home-made
   (see page 30) or ready-made, cut into
   2.5-cm/1-inch cubes

To garnish

A small handful of coriander (cilantro) leaves

A few green chillis, left whole or roughly
   chopped (optional)

In a frying pan (skillet) or wok, heat the oil over a medium–high heat. Add the sliced onion to the pan and fry gently, stirring occasionally, until golden brown and caramelized (see page 11). Using a slotted spoon, remove the onion from the oil, leaving as much of the oil in the pan as possible to cook the other ingredients, and place on a plate to drain. Spread the onions across the plate so they crisp as they cool.

Add the diced bell pepper to the pan, followed by the tomato, ginger and garlic pastes, chilli powder, ground turmeric, ground coriander, salt and yogurt. Cook over a high heat, stirring continuously, for 5 minutes. Add the diced paneer to the pan and stir to coat the paneer in the masala. Cook for a further few minutes. Taste to check the seasoning and adjust as necessary.

Before serving, garnish with the coriander leaves and green chillis, if preferred. If you do not want to make the dish spicier, keep the chillis whole. If you want to add some extra heat, roughly chop the chillis.

Learning from stories

Most of the cooks in my family home learnt the recipes for specific dishes like an oral history. Some did not write well and felt it was unnecessary to note down their recipes. One of the men who taught me to cook had a cataract and was almost totally blind, so he could not see to read or write a recipe. His way of teaching how long to fry onions for was by telling me that 'the onions need to look like pearls'. He would describe how something should look or smell when ready, and would encourage me to link it to a memory with a similar feeling. Recipes were taught in same way as stories, rather than through prescriptive instructions. The cook would recount the sights and sounds that I needed to look out for – it was like listening to a tale being told – and almost without even realizing, I came out of that session in the kitchen having learnt a recipe.

I have never forgotten any of the dishes I was taught in this way. You may forget recipes, but you don't forget stories. I feel very lucky to have had that learning experience. In the same way, in sharing some of my food tales with you, I hope that you begin to see recipes not as a list of rules, but rather as a series of moments. Remember, you are the creator of every dish. It is your touch, with your unique fingerprints, that will bring a dish to life. Although, I am here to hold your hand all the way.

Saag Paneer
Spinach with Indian cheese V

Eaten with bread or rice, Saag Paneer makes a satisfying midweek meal. Spinach is one of those vegetables that can be hard to estimate as it reduces dramatically when cooked. As this recipe is a main dish for two adults, I've suggested 750–900 g/1 lb 10 oz–2 lb of spinach, which will cook down to about 2 cups. Paneer is readily available in supermarkets, although should you want to make your own, I have given a simple recipe on page 30. My personal preference is not to fry the paneer before it is added to this dish, but if you prefer to give the paneer cubes a little colour then follow the frying instructions on page 85.

Serves 2

750–900 g/1 lb 10 oz–2 lb fresh spinach, washed

2 tbsp melted ghee, butter or vegetable oil

2 shallots, finely chopped

½ tsp fresh ginger paste

2 garlic cloves, crushed

1 tomato, chopped into cubes

1 green chilli, cut in half

¼ tsp ground turmeric

¼ tsp chilli powder

Salt to taste

100 g/3½ oz paneer, home-made (see page 30) or ready-made, cut into 2.5-cm/1-inch cubes

1 tbsp double (heavy) cream or clotted cream

Bring a large pan of water to the boil. Drop the spinach into the pan and blanch for 20–30 seconds. Using a slotted spoon, remove the spinach from the pan, drain and refresh in cold water. Roughly chop the spinach, then squeeze to remove any remaining liquid – it should be as dry as possible.

In a shallow saucepan, heat the ghee, butter or oil over a medium heat. Add the chopped shallots, ginger paste and garlic and cook for 2 minutes until they start to colour.

Add the diced tomato, green chilli, ground turmeric, chilli powder and salt. Cook over a medium–high heat for 5–6 minutes. Add the blanched spinach and paneer cubes. Cook, stirring, for a further 3–4 minutes.

Taste to check the seasoning and adjust as necessary. Before serving, pour the cream over the top of the dish.

Hari Phoolgobi
Broccoli with nigella seeds and egg V

Broccoli is not readily available in India, so there is no Hindi word for it. Literally translated, Hari Phoolgobi means 'green cauliflower'. In India cauliflowers are smaller than those you find in the West. The first time I saw broccoli I thought it was what an Indian cauliflower would look like if it became super-sized and turned green... like the Hulk! This is an adaptation of a cauliflower dish my family cook made in India. I suspect his intention with his recipe was to get us kids to eat more vegetables, with the eggs acting as camouflage. As this recipe is for two, I am not giving an exact weight for the broccoli; instead, estimate by sight whether or not a head of broccoli is large enough.

Serves 2

1 head of broccoli (approximately 350 g/12 oz)

2 tbsp vegetable oil

¼ tsp nigella (black onion) seeds

2 dried red chillis, broken in half

¼ tsp ground turmeric

4 medium eggs, beaten

½ tsp salt

Break up the head of broccoli into individual florets. Bring a large pan of water to the boil. Drop the florets into the pan and cook for 2 minutes. Using a slotted spoon, remove the broccoli from the pan, drain and refresh in cold water. Keep the water used for boiling the broccoli in case it is needed later to prevent sticking.

In a frying pan (skillet), heat the vegetable oil over a medium–high heat. Add the nigella seeds and dried red chillis to the pan and cook, stirring, until the chillis start to darken. Next, add the broccoli florets and season with salt. Add the ground turmeric to the pan, then pour the beaten eggs over the broccoli and add the salt. Cook, stirring continuously, for no more than 5 minutes – the egg should scramble and cling to the florets. If the egg or any of the spices stick to the base of the pan, add a splash of the broccoli cooking water.

Taste to check the seasoning and adjust as necessary.

Anda Curry
Hard-boiled eggs in gravy V

Eggs are the fall-back ingredient in every Indian household. I associate egg curry with monsoons in Calcutta, when the bazaar was closed due to flooding. The local delivery man would bring eggs to our home, cycling through the flooded streets. The egg curry made at home usually included potatoes to make the dish more substantial, though I have omitted them here. You can use any type of egg for this dish, even quail eggs. In India we leave the eggs whole, but you can halve them before returning them to the pan. Just be careful not to lose their yolks in the gravy.

Serves 2

4 medium eggs

6 tbsp vegetable oil

1 green cardamom pod

1 clove

1 Indian bay leaf

½ tsp cumin seeds

2 medium onions, finely chopped

1 tsp garlic paste

1 tbsp fresh ginger paste

½ tsp ground turmeric

1 tbsp ground coriander

½ tsp chilli powder

6 tbsp natural (plain) yogurt

1 tsp salt

A handful of fresh herbs, to garnish

If you keep your eggs in the refrigerator, take them out 30 minutes before cooking to bring them to room temperature. Fill a large pan with water and bring to a rolling boil over a high heat. Lower the heat to a simmer, then place the eggs in the water and cook for 12 minutes. Using a slotted spoon, remove the eggs from the pan and place in cold running water to prevent further cooking. When cool enough to handle, shell the eggs.

In a shallow saucepan, heat the oil over a medium–high heat. Add the hard-boiled eggs and cook until they are speckled all over with brown patches. Remove the eggs from the pan and set aside.

To the remaining oil, add the cardamom, clove and bay leaf. Add the cumin seeds and cook, stirring, for a few seconds until the seeds darken.

Add the chopped onions, garlic and ginger to the pan, cook for a further 5 minutes until the onion mixture has softened and coloured to a light brown. Continue to stir while cooking to prevent the onions from burning and sticking to the base of the pan. If the onion mixture does stick to the base of the pan, sprinkle over some water.

Add the ground turmeric, coriander and chilli powder. Cook, stirring, for 10–20 seconds or until the 'raw' smell of the turmeric has disappeared, taking care not to let the ground spices burn. Pour over 200 ml/7 fl oz/¾ cup plus 1 tbsp cold water and increase the heat to high. Once any excess water has evaporated, lower the heat.

To avoid any lumps in the sauce, stir the yogurt before adding it to the pan. Stir to mix evenly and then season with salt. Lastly, add the hard-boiled eggs to the pan and allow to heat through before serving.

Before serving, scatter over plenty of fresh herbs.

Masoor Dal
Red lentils V

This basic dal recipe can be adapted to your own taste by adding extra ingredients to the lentils, such as handfuls of chopped spinach or chunks of fresh tomato. The tempering is a very important final stage in making dal as so much flavour is contained in that spiced oil, which is poured over the cooked lentils. This recipe makes a generous amount fot two people with leftovers that can be reheated in a pan the next day: a smaller quantity of lentils would end up sticking to the base of the pan.

Serves 2

500 g/1 lb 2 oz /2½ cups masoor dal
   (red lentils)

2 tbsp ghee or oil

3–4 dried red chillis

1 small onion, finely chopped

4 garlic cloves, finely chopped

1½ tsp salt

1 tsp ground turmeric

For the tempering

2 tbsp ghee or oil

2 dried red chillis

½ tsp cumin seeds

1 garlic clove, cut into slivers

4 fresh curry leaves

Wash the lentils in cold running water, then place in a bowl and soak for 30 minutes in fresh cold water. (If you do not have time to soak the lentils, then just wash them before adding to the pan – red lentils cook quickly and so do not need long soaking.)

In a heavy-based pan that has a lid, heat 2 tbsp of oil or ghee over a medium–high heat. Add the dried red chillis to the pan, followed by the minced onion and garlic. Cook, stirring, until they just start to colour.

Add the soaked lentils to the pan, then the salt and ground turmeric. Add 1.2 litres/2 pints/10 cups warm water to the lentils and bring to the boil. When the surface of the water is bubbling, cover the pan, lower the heat and simmer gently for 30 minutes. Stir occasionally to ensure the dal is not sticking to the base of the pan. Once the dal is cooked, place it in a bowl and keep warm while preparing the tempering.

In a small frying pan (skillet), heat the remaining 2 tbsp of ghee or oil over a high heat. Working very quickly so the tempering does not burn, add the dried red chillis, cumin seeds, garlic slivers and, finally, the curry leaves. Cook for a few seconds, then pour the tempering oil and spices over the warm dal in the pan. Next, take a spoonful of the dal and place it in the frying pan to absorb any remaining oil – take care whilst doing this as the oil may splutter – then tip the spoonful of dal from the frying pan back into the main dal pan.

Serve immediately, ladling the dal into separate serving bowls.

Tamatar Bharta
Smoky mashed tomatoes V

The smokiness that comes from cooking over open flames or charring on coal embers adds a wonderful extra dimension to any dish. The best way to char the tomatoes for this recipe is to place them directly on a heat source, however this is not always the most practical method. Grilling or oven roasting the tomatoes is easier and less messy. Make sure the heat is set to low–medium so the tomatoes cook all the way through.

Serves 2

2 medium–large tomatoes

½ tsp lime juice

½ tsp mustard oil (or argan oil)

1 green chilli, chopped

1 garlic clove, bashed and finely chopped

¼ tsp salt (adjust to taste)

The tomatoes can be cooked either in the oven or under the grill (broiler). The cooking times for tomatoes will vary depending on their variety, size and water content, so do keep checking during the cooking.

If cooking in an oven, preheat the oven to 160°C/325°F/Gas Mark 3. Place the whole tomatoes in an oven tray and slow roast for 20–30 minutes. As the tomatoes dehydrate, they will lose their shape and collapse – this is when you know they are almost ready. When the tomatoes reach this stage, turn off the heat and leave them in oven for a further 10 minutes. When ready, the skins should be charred and the flesh cooked all the way through.

Once cooked, place the tomatoes in a bowl and leave until they are cool enough to handle. Remove the charred tomato skins and then, using kitchen scissors, chop the tomato flesh into small pieces.

Add all the remaining ingredients to the bowl of chopped tomatoes and mix to combine. Taste to check the seasoning and adjust as necessary.

If you make the bharta in advance, remember that the intensity of the chilli will increase over time as it infuses in the tomato mixture.

Baingan Aloo
Aubergine with potatoes <u>v</u>

This is a moist vegetable dish that can be eaten with any kind of bread or rice; I often serve this on thick slices of sourdough toast... Delicious! Standard white or waxy potatoes work best for this recipe, rather than floury potatoes that will fall apart while cooking. Depending on the variety, quality and size of potatoes used, you may need to adjust the cooking time.

Serves 2

1 large or 4 small aubergines (eggplants) (approximately 1 kg/2 lb 4 oz)

2 medium potatoes (standard white potatoes, such as Maris Piper, approximately 600 g/ 1 lb 6 oz), peeled

½ tsp ground turmeric

1 tsp salt

Vegetable oil, for frying

1 garlic clove, crushed to a paste

1 tsp grated fresh ginger

1 fresh green chilli, cut into 1-cm/½-inch pieces

1 tomato, cut into wedges

A pinch of sugar

A handful of coriander (cilantro) leaves, chopped, to garnish

Cut the aubergines and potatoes into thick wedges that are equal in size. Place the wedges on a plate, sprinkle over the ground turmeric and ¼ tsp of the salt. Set aside for 30 minutes.

In a large frying pan (skillet), heat 2 tbsp oil over a medium–high heat. Add the aubergine wedges and fry on each side for 1 minute. Using a slotted spoon, remove the aubergine wedges to a plate and set aside. Lower the heat and then, in the same pan, fry the potato wedges. Cook until the potatoes are a crusty brown on the outside, but not cooked all the way through. Remove the potato wedges to a plate and set aside.

In a large pan, heat 1 tbsp oil over a medium–high heat. Add the crushed garlic, ginger and green chilli and cook, stirring, for 1 minute. Add the tomato wedges with the pinch of sugar and remaining salt, then return the aubergine and potato wedges to the pan. Cook over a high heat for a further minute, then cover and lower the heat to medium and cook for 5 minutes.

After 5 minutes, check the potatoes are cooked through. Do not add any water to the pan while cooking; the liquid from the aubergines and tomatoes will be enough to cook the potatoes.

Taste to check the seasoning and adjust as necessary. Before serving, garnish with chopped coriander leaves.

Masala Omelette v

A quick and easy meal, this dish requires minimum preparation and can be served with either paratha or even toast. If you are cooking for one, still make two omelettes – one to enjoy straight away and the second to make into a sandwich the next day. Call me old-fashioned, but I strongly believe a Masala Omelette sandwich must be made with white bread and salted butter. Tomato ketchup is equally important. Enjoy with a glass of Adrak Masala (see page 57).

Serves 2

4 medium eggs

2 green chillis

2 spring onions (scallions), finely chopped

4 tbsp finely chopped tomatoes

4 tbsp chopped coriander (cilantro) leaves
  (or any other herb)

¼ tsp freshly ground black pepper

½ tsp salt (adjust to taste)

2 tbsp melted butter or oil

For an omelette sandwich

A couple of slices of white bread

Plenty of salted butter

A good squeeze of tomato ketchup

In a bowl, beat the eggs. If you prefer not to eat the green chillis, chop them into pieces large enough to see so that you can remove them later. If you enjoy eating chillis, finely chop them. Add the chopped chillis to the beaten eggs in the bowl along with all the other ingredients, except the butter or oil.

In a small non-stick frying pan (skillet), heat 1 tbsp of the butter or oil over a medium heat. Add half the egg mixture to the pan and leave to 'set' before gently folding the omelette over to cook through.

Slide the omelette from the pan onto a plate and keep warm. Repeat for the second omelette.

To make the omelette sandwich, butter two slices of white bread with a generous amount of salted butter. Place the folded omelette on top of one slice of buttered bread. Squeeze a generous amount of tomato ketchup over the omelette filling before covering with the second slice of buttered bread.

Palak Gosht
Meat with spinach

This dish can be made with any kind of meat, but preferably a cut that is on the bone, such as lamb shanks or chicken thighs, as it will have so much more flavour than meat off the bone.

However, there is one exception to this rule. If you are serving this dish as part of a family-style sharing meal – especially if your guests will be standing while eating – it may be more practical to use boneless meat pieces. If using beef, try chuck steak, or if using lamb, try leg or shoulder, and then dice the meat into 5-cm/2-inch cubes.

This dish tastes even better the next day, so I prefer to make it the day before I serve it – even though the spinach will look darker after a night in the refrigerator. For storing, use a plastic box with an airtight lid to keep the food moist and trap those spicy aromas!

Serves 6–8

4 tbsp vegetable oil

1 piece cassia bark, 4 cm/1½ inches long (see page 13)

3 cloves

3 green cardamom pods

1 Indian bay leaf

1 dried red chillis

2 small onions, finely chopped then crushed to a paste

4 garlic cloves, crushed to a paste

1 tbsp fresh ginger paste

1 green chilli, cut in half

750–900 g/1 lb 10 oz–2 lb meat of your choice, such as lamb shanks or skinless, bone-in chicken thighs

½ tsp ground turmeric

½ tbsp ground coriander

½ tbsp ground cumin

1 tomato, diced

1 tbsp full-fat natural (plain) yogurt

½ tsp salt (adjust to taste)

400 g/14 oz fresh spinach, cooked and squeezed dry or 200 g/7 oz frozen spinach, squeezed dry

In a heavy-based pan that has a lid, heat the oil over a medium–high heat. Add the cassia bark, cloves, cardamom pods, bay leaves and dried red chillis. Stir until the chillis have darkened in colour. Using a slotted spoon, remove the spices and chillis from the pan, place on a plate and set aside.

In the same pan and using the chilli-infused oil, fry the lamb shanks or chicken thighs until brown on all sides. Do not allow the meat to cook through; the aim is just to seal the meat. Remove the meat from the pan and set aside, leaving as much of the oil in the pan as possible.

Add the onion, garlic, green chilli and ginger paste to the pan. Take care as the paste will sputter in the hot oil. Next, add the ground turmeric, ground coriander and ground cumin. If the lamb shanks weigh more than 900 g/ 2 lb, add an additionl pinch of each ground spice. Increase the heat to high and add the diced tomatoes and cook for 2 minutes before adding the yogurt.

Return the whole fried spices, dried chillis and sealed meat to the pan. Add the salt, cover with 750 ml/1¼ pints/3 cups water and bring to the boil. After 1 minute, cover the pan with the lid and lower the heat to a simmer. The cooking time will vary according to the type of meat you are using. For lamb shanks, simmer for 2 hours and for chicken thighs simmer for 1 hour.

Once the meat is cooked, remove the lid, add the spinach and reduce any remaining liquid until the oil seeps to the edges of the pan.

Chicken Bharta
Shredded chicken with eggs in gravy

Some of the best places to eat Punjabi food in Calcutta were the dhabas, no-frills roadside restaurants where the clientele was mostly discerning taxi and truck drivers. Chicken Bharta was unique to these dhabas, combining the rich butter chicken of North India with the Bengali love for eggs and bhortas (a dish of mashed-up vegetables fried with spices, see page 20). Although a long walk from our house, it was a treat for the family to go to our favourite dhaba, opposite Kwality in the Ballygunge, for Chicken Bharta. Few dhabas are still in existence in Calcutta: the Ballygunge dhaba closed suddenly last year. While I cannot recreate the distinctive sights and sounds of that dhaba, I have tried to replicate the iconic Chicken Bharta served there.

Serves 2

4 large skinless, bone-in chicken thighs (approximately 500 g/1 lb 2 oz)

1 tbsp vegetable oil

1 Indian bay leaf

1 dried red chilli

½ tsp kasuri methi (dried fenugreek leaves)

2 cloves

1 piece cassia bark, 1 cm/½ inch long

1 large onion, finely chopped

1 tomato, chopped

1 tbsp fresh ginger paste

½ tbsp garlic paste

2 green chillis, chopped

½ tsp ground turmeric

1 tsp ground garam masala (see page 14)

½ tsp sugar

1 tbsp cashew nut paste

½ tbsp char magaz (melon seed) paste

2 tbsp full-fat natural (plain) yogurt

3 eggs, hard-boiled, peeled and with yolks and whites separated

1½ tbsp double (heavy) cream

1 tsp unsalted butter

Place the chicken thighs in a large pan that has a lid, cover with cold water, add ½ tsp salt and then bring to the boil over a high heat. Once boiling, lower the heat, cover with the lid and simmer for 15 minutes.

Once cooked, remove the chicken from the pan onto a plate and leave until it is cool enough to handle. Do not throw away the cooking water in which the chicken has been boiled, it will be used later. While still warm, pull the chicken thigh meat off the bone and shred into thick strips.

Heat the oil in a heavy-based pan over a medium–high heat. Add the bay leaf, dried red chilli, kasuri methi, cloves and cassia bark and cook, stirring, for 1 minute. Next, add the onion and stir for another minute. Now add the tomato, ginger and garlic pastes and chopped green chillis. Cook for 10–15 minutes or until the oil separates from the mixture.

To the pan, add the ground turmeric and garam masala followed by the sugar and 1 tsp salt. Cook for 1–2 minutes over a low heat. Next, add the cashew nut paste, char magaz paste and yogurt. Cook until the water in the yogurt has evaporated and any oil has seeped to the edges.

Add the shredded chicken to the pan and stir to coat the strips of meat with the mixture. Mash the hard-boiled egg yolks with a fork and add to the pan, followed by 240 ml/1 cup of the warm cooking water in which the chicken was poached. Cook for a further 15–20 minutes, then once the sauce has thickened, remove the pan from the heat, add the cream and butter before gently stirring.

Slice the hard-boiled egg whites into wedges and scatter over the dish to garnish. Serve immediately and eat while hot with any bread or salad.

Sukhi Bhindi
Sautéed okra with garlic <u>V</u>

Okra is often called 'ladies' fingers' in India. Quite disturbing, when you think about a woman with green fingers that shape. Okra is readily available in supermarkets. If you buy okra from a market, look for lighter, thinner green okra. Be sure not to buy the larger, thicker African variety as it contains a lot more sap and will not work in this recipe.

Serves 2

250–300 g/9–10½ oz okra
4 tbsp vegetable oil
4 garlic cloves, crushed
¼ tsp ground turmeric
¼ tsp chilli powder
¼ tsp salt
1 tbsp lemon juice

Rinse the okra in cold water, then dry with a clean dish towel to remove any additional moisture that will make the dish soggy. Top and tail the okra, then slice them diagonally into 2.5-cm/1-inch pieces.

In a frying pan (skillet), heat the oil over a medium heat. Add the crushed garlic to the pan and sauté for 1 minute – do not allow the garlic to become crisp and brown. Add the okra slices to the pan with the ground turmeric, chilli powder and salt. Increase the heat to high and cook, uncovered, while stirring gently so as not to bruise the okra. The okra should cook in less than 5 minutes; it should be tender, but not soft, and still have some bite.

Sprinkle the lemon juice over the okra and then take the pan off the heat. Taste to check the seasoning and adjust as necessary.

Macher Malaikari
Fish in coconut milk

For a long time I was under the impression that the name of this dish derived from the Hindi word 'malai', meaning cream. Recently, however, I discovered that the origin of this creamy, coconut-based fish curry may be a little more 'foreign'. During colonial rule, this dish was made in the Malay Peninsula by Bengali labourers who were sent there by the British to build the railways. Coconut milk is frequently used in East Asian cuisine, but rarely in Bengali dishes. The fact that this dish was once called 'Malaya-Kari' explains the use of coconut milk, as opposed to mustard and mustard oil, which is the more common base for fish and seafood dishes in Bengal.

Serves 2 as a main course or
4 as part of a multi-course meal

4 halibut, plaice or tilapia fillets
    (approximately 750 g/1 lb 10 oz)
1 tsp ground turmeric
1 tsp salt
3 tbsp vegetable oil
2 large white onions, thinly sliced into half
    moons
1 tbsp garlic paste
1½ tbsp fresh ginger paste
¼ tsp chilli powder
1 tbsp tomato purée (tomato paste)
1 x 400-ml/14-fl oz tin full-fat coconut milk
A pinch of sugar

To garnish
Green chillis, finely sliced
Coriander (cilantro) leaves, chopped

Place the fish fillets on a plate, sprinkle over half the ground turmeric and half the salt and rub into the fillets. Leave for a minimum of 10 minutes but no longer than 30 minutes.

In a heavy-based frying pan (skillet), heat the oil over a medium–high heat. Add the sliced onions to the pan and fry gently, stirring occasionally, until golden brown and caramelized (see page 11). Using a slotted spoon, remove the onions from the pan, leaving as much of the oil in the pan as possible to cook the other ingredients, and place on a plate to drain. Spread the onions across the plate so they crisp as they cool.

You should have enough oil left in the pan to fry the fish; if not, add another 1 tbsp vegetable oil. In the same pan, flash-fry the fish fillets for 20–30 seconds on both sides to seal. Do not allow the fish to cook. Remove the fish from the pan and set aside on a plate.

Keeping the heat at medium–high, add the garlic and ginger pastes to the pan and cook, stirring, for 1 minute. Add the remaining ground turmeric and the chilli powder. If the pastes stick to the base of the pan, sprinkle over some water. Add the tomato purée, 4 tbsp warm water, the remaining salt and the fried onions, then cook for few minutes until the oil has seeped to the edges of the pan.

Return the fish fillets to the pan and cook for a further 2 minutes. Add the coconut milk, then immediately remove the pan from the heat and carefully turn each fillet over. Taste the coconut milk and adjust the seasoning with sugar or salt as necessary. Before serving, garnish with sliced green chillis and chopped coriander.

Phali Ki Sabzi
Green beans with cumin seeds V

It was only while writing this book I realized how difficult it is to find a generic Hindi word for green beans. The most commonly cooked green beans in India are gawar ki phalli, which grow in clusters, are thinner and taste more bitter than other green beans. Flat beans, known as seem, looks a little like broad beans but have a thicker skin and tough edge (possibly as protection from the harsh sun). Seem always remind me of our family cook, Islam, who loved growing vegetables. He was traumatized at leaving our home in Hyderabad, where he spent most of his day gardening, to move to a smaller house in Calcutta, where the adjoining building plunged most of our garden into shade. But in the small patches of earth that did catch the sun, Islam would grow seem. He gave each plant so much care, they all produced a huge quantity of beans. When Islam died, as if on cue, the plants withered away. The real reason was probably because none of the other cooks bothered to water the plants, but as a child I was convinced that the beans died because they were broken-hearted over the loss of Islam.

Serves 2

250 g/9 oz green beans (any variety will work as long as the beans are all the same size so they cook evenly)

1 tbsp ghee or vegetable oil

¼ tsp cumin seeds (or use mustard seeds or sesame seeds)

2 garlic cloves, finely chopped

1 dried red chilli, broken in half

¼ tsp ground turmeric

Salt, to taste

Trim the ends of the beans. If using fine green beans, remove any stringy fibres. If using runner beans, cut them into 2.5-cm/ 1-inch pieces.

Heat the ghee or oil in a deep pan or wok over a medium–high heat, add the cumin seeds and wait for them to darken. Add the garlic, dried red chilli and ground turmeric, followed by the green beans. Add salt to taste and stir fry until the beans are cooked through, but still crunchy.

———

The beans can be cooked in advance and reheated just before serving. If reheating, slightly undercook the beans when preparing the dish.

Rogni Roti
Enriched unleavened bread <u>V</u>

The origin of this wholemeal roti is clear from its name: 'Rogni' is derived from the Persian word Rogan (روغن), which means clarified butter or fat. The Persian influence on Indian cuisine goes as far back as the thirteenth century and its impact was most evident during the Mughal period, from the sixteenth to the nineteenth centuries.

Rogni Roti is bread made in the Bulandshahr district in Uttar Pradesh, northern India. In my family, we call it 'Safar Roti', or bread for travelling. Traditionally families in North India eat mainly wheat and, as the trusty sandwich (the Western alternative to bread you can eat on the move) was not an option in the sixteenth and seventeenth centuries, someone came up with this bread recipe.

Made with wholemeal or chapati flour and enriched with milk and ghee or oil, this bread is cooked in a different way, which allows the bread to remain crisp on the outside and soft on the inside when cold – a perfect bread to take on a journey. My childhood memory of this bread is travelling to visit our extended family, living in the villages in Bulandshahr, and on train journeys to Delhi. In summer, we usually ate the bread with achaar (pickle) or chutney, boiled eggs and local cucumbers. In winter, I remember having a simple potato and cumin dish with the Rogni Roti.

This roti stays fresh for several hours. Our family cook makes Rogni Roti for me to snack on during the car journey of several hours from my parents' home in Aligargh to Delhi airport.

Makes 6

225 g/8 oz/1¾ cups wholemeal (whole wheat) or chapati flour

½ tsp salt

8 tbsp whole milk

50 g/2 oz/4 tbsp melted ghee or butter, plus an extra 25 g/1 oz/2 tbsp for cooking

Place the flour and salt in a large mixing bowl. Make a well in the centre of the flour and pour in the milk and melted ghee or butter. Mix all the ingredients together with your hands until they come together to form a moist dough. On a lightly floured work surface, knead the dough until firm. If the dough is too dry, add a splash of milk.

If you do not plan to cook the roti straightaway, divide the dough into six equal pieces, place the dough in a plastic container covered with a lid and store in the refrigerator for up to two days.

When ready to cook the roti, roll each piece into a flat 13-cm/5-inch disc. Using a fork, prick each flattened roti all over.

Heat a tawa (flat iron griddle pan) or non-stick frying pan (skillet) over a medium–high heat. Grease the pan with more melted ghee or butter, then cook the roti in batches on both sides. Using scrunched-up paper towels, press each roti down in the pan until brown.

The roti can be eaten either warm or cool. Once cool, wrap the roti in foil and store at room temperature for several hours.

'Why did you call your food business after a train?'

That is a question I am often asked. Darjeeling Express is a meter gauge steam train that runs along the Himalayan foothills, ferrying holidaymakers from the plains in Calcutta to the mountains in Darjeeling. In April 2012, I arrived home in London after completing my law PhD viva exams with the knowledge that I had passed my PhD. After the initial hours of exhilaration, I was certain that I did not want to teach law. Instead, I decided that I was going to start a food business. That night, I registered my business online and was not expecting to be asked for a name by the system – after all, I had never done this before. I wrote the first thing that came to my mind: Darjeeling Express. The train journeys I made on the Darjeeling Express as a child are joyous memories. They were an escape from the sweltering city heat of Calcutta. As the train made its slow and laboured journey along the mountains, huffing and puffing, I sat enthralled, watching the scenery. As we took a turn along the mountain edge, I remember putting my face against the train window and calling out my own name only to hear the mountains echo it back to me. I felt completely in control of my world – liberated, but in charge of my destiny. I imagined I was driving the train and the mountains were calling out my name to greet me. Decades later, as I sat in my London home with my son by my side, I was taken back to that moment of liberation and joy, of childhood fantasies and imagination. My Darjeeling Express moment had come. Finally, I was driving that iconic train along the spectacular mountain path.

Spiced Himalayan Tea <u>V</u>

For this spiced tea recipe, I prefer to use second flush Darjeeling tea. Often the second flush tea is considered the poor relative of the first flush, which is highly unfair. Both varieties have their own distinct properties. The lightness of a first flush tea bud, picked at dawn during the earliest part of the season, has its own particular beauty. Second flush tea, which is picked later in the season after the leaves have had time to mature, has a much greater depth and colour. Here, a stronger tea that can counterbalance all the spices is needed, but you can experiment using other lighter black teas.

Serves 2

1 piece fresh ginger, 5-mm/¼-inch long, cut into small pieces (you can leave the skin on)

6 tbsp light brown sugar

1 piece cassia bark, 1 cm/½ inch long (see page 13)

6 green cardamom pods

6 cloves

2 Indian bay leaves

½ tsp black peppercorns

2 tbsp second flush loose-leaf Darjeeling tea

250 ml/8½ fl oz/1 cup whole milk

Pour 1.5 litres/2¾ pints/6¼ cups water into a large pan that has a lid and bring to the boil over a high heat. Once boiling, add the ginger, sugar and all the spices and bring back to the boil. Lower the heat to a simmer, cover with a lid and leave for 30 minutes.

Remove the lid and bring the water back to a slow, rolling boil for 15 minutes. Add the loose-leaf tea and milk and keep the contents of the pan on a slow, rolling boil. Taste and adjust the sweetness with more sugar, if required. If the teas is too sweet, add more milk.

Take the pan off the heat, strain the tea and serve while hot.

———

Use a pan that is large enough for the water to boil – you do not want to waste your time cleaning spills from your cooker!

Adrak Masala
Chai-spiced ginger tea V

Use strong black tea when making this beverage, such as Kenyan or Assam Orthodox. Loose-leaf tea is best, but otherwise use any strong black teabag.

Serves 2

250 ml/8½ fl oz/1 cup whole milk

5-mm/¼-inch piece fresh ginger, cut into small pieces

50 g/1¾ oz/¼ cup soft light brown sugar

1 piece cassia bark, 2.5 cm/1 inch long (see page 13)

6 green cardamom pods

6 cloves

2 tbsp loose-leaf strong black tea

Pour the milk and 1.5 litres/2¾ pints/6¼ cups water into a large pan and bring to the boil over a high heat. Once boiling, add the ginger, sugar and all the spices. Lower the heat to a low boil then leave, uncovered, for 20 minutes.

After 20 minutes, add the loose-leaf tea. Increase the heat until the liquid is boiling vigorously. After 1 minute, lower the heat and allow the tea to simmer for 2 minutes. For the final minute, increase the heat to high and boil the tea on full.

Take the pan off the heat, strain the tea and serve while hot.

Fruit Chaat <u>v</u>

This fresh fruit dessert is a colourful way to end a meal. Fruit Chaat is very popular in India and is sold on the streets as well as being made at home. There are many versions of this chaat recipe; there are no hard-and-fast rules on what goes into a Fruit Chaat. I have one rule: always add pineapples! In Calcutta, diced pineapples are served with a sprinkling of kala namak (Himalayan rock salt) – a flavouring that I love. Since living in England, I have experimented and added brown sugar and lime juice to the fruits, which gives a tangy and sweet flavouring to the chaat. Be careful with the Himalayan rock salt though; the pink version sold in some supermarkets is not as pungent as the salt bought in Indian grocery stores.

Serves 2

1 punnet strawberries, raspberries or blueberries

1 kiwi fruit, apple or pear

1 small bunch grapes

1 orange

1 small pineapple (buy ready-peeled for ease)

1 tbsp pomegranate seeds (optional)

1 tbsp brown sugar

2 tbsp lime juice

A generous pinch of Himalayan rock salt (adjust to taste)

Slice the strawberries and kiwis. Slice any other berries and grapes in half. Peel the orange and cut into segments. Cut all the other fruits into even 2.5-cm/1-inch cubes. Place all the fruit along with the pomegranate seeds in a bowl.

In a small pan, dissolve the sugar in the lime juice over a low heat. Pour over the prepared fruits in the bowl. Cautiously add the Himalayan rock salt to the fruit.

Before serving, taste to check the seasoning and adjust as necessary.

Family Feasts

'My Mama is a yucky cook.'

That was my younger son's first full written sentence at school, aged 4, when asked to write one line to describe his mother. While my older son has always loved spices and been willing to try new dishes, my younger son really disliked the smell of masalas, especially haldi (turmeric), and was never willing to taste Indian food. I did give him dals while weaning but once he got a bit older, he would refuse to eat anything that smelt of any spice. I did not want mealtimes to become a battleground, so I did not try to force him into eating the same food as the rest of the family.

This situation with my son, Fariz, eventually became awkward when I took him to visit my parents and in-laws in the Indian sub-continent. It was hard to deal with the comments about my 'English boy' who ate no spice! The worst moments were the big family feasts, when my son was unwilling to try anything new. My son would loudly exclaim, 'I am not eating anything yellow,' and then continue to add, 'Or anything brown!' I think every family gathering has a Fariz in it, so in this chapter on Family Feasts I have included recipes that are proven crowd pleasers. These are recipes that look good and are packed with flavour – inviting dishes for even the hesitant Indian-food eater. These are the recipes that finally encouraged my son to eat Indian food. There is a misconception that all Indian food is fiery and packed with chillis, but that simply isn't true. Chilli is just one spice and the recipes suitable for all generations at a family feast balance that chilli flavour with other herbs and spices, such as cinnamon, cumin and saffron.

Peela Pulao
Lemon rice with cashew nuts V

I remember eating Peela Pulao as a child, when we lived in Chennai. Islam was our family cook, who stayed with us for decades, even after we moved back to Calcutta, refusing to retire despite his advancing years and fading eyesight. Islam frequently made this lemon rice dish for us. Mustard seeds are used extensively in Bengali cooking, although are not as common in rice dishes, so it may have been the influence of South Indian ingredients that led him to magic up this recipe. While mustard seeds, curry leaves and cashew nuts all hail from the south, this rice dish perfectly complements many North Indian dishes. (See page 44 for photograph, served with Palak Gosht.) Nuts were not readily available in all regions of India, so the addition of cashew nuts, which are grown in the south, elevates this rice recipe from a humble everyday staple to a dish that would impress any guest at a feast.

Serves 6

300 g/10½ oz/1½ cups basmati rice

3 tbsp vegetable oil

2 green cardamom pods

1 piece cassia bark, 2.5 cm/1 inch long
   (see page 13)

2 whole cloves

1 large Indian bay leaf

1 medium white onion, evenly and thinly sliced
   into rings

1 tsp black mustard seeds

1 tbsp cashew nuts

10 curry leaves

1 tsp ground turmeric

1½ tsp salt

Juice of 1 lemon, plus the zest cut into slivers

Wash the basmati rice in several changes of cold running water until the water runs clear, then place in a bowl and soak for 2 hours in more fresh cold water. (If you do not have time to soak the rice for 2 hours, then do soak it for as long as possible before cooking – even the briefest soaking time makes a difference.)

When ready to cook, drain the soaked basmati rice and set aside. In a heavy-based pan that has a lid, heat the oil over a medium–high heat. When the oil is hot, add the cardamom pods, cassia bark, cloves and bay leaf to the pan. After a few seconds, when the spices begin to sizzle and pop, using a slotted spoon, remove them from the pan to a plate and set aside.

Using the same oil the spices were fried in, add the onion rings to the pan and fry gently, stirring occasionally, until golden brown and caramelized (see page 11). Using a slotted spoon, remove the onions from the pan, leaving as much of the oil in the pan as possible to cook the other ingredients, and place on a plate to drain. Spread the onion rings across the plate so they crisp as they cool.

Put the kettle on to boil. You should have enough oil left in the pan to fry the spices and cashew nuts; if not, add another 1 tbsp vegetable oil. To the same pan, add the mustard seeds and fry until they pop, then add the cashew nuts and curry leaves. Immediately add the soaked rice and ground turmeric to the pan. Stir for 1 minute to coat the rice in the spice-infused oil, then cover the rice with 600 ml/ 1 pint/2½ cups boiling water from the kettle.

Return the fried whole spices and caramelized onion rings to the pan in the rice water. Add the salt. Cook uncovered over a medium–high heat until the water has been almost absorbed by the rice (about 4 minutes).

Once most of the water has been absorbed, add half the lemon zest slivers. Cover the pan with the lid, lower the heat and simmer for a further 15–20 minutes. Once the rice is cooked, pour the lemon juice into the rice and gently mix using a fork to lift and separate the grains.

To serve, garnish the rice with the remaining lemon zest slivers.

Murgh Rezala
Aromatic chicken stew

Rezala shares similarities with Persian stew. An unusual chicken dish, it is made only in certain regions of India, which had historical trading relations with the Persians. Mild and fragrant, this version of Rezala is made in both Bengal, India and Bangladesh. The kick of green chillis is very subtle. The use of freshly squeezed lemon juice in the dish is possibly an adaptation by Indians who most likely found Persian preserved lemons too tangy for their palette. Mild enough for children to eat, this is a good dish to prepare when cooking for the whole family.

Serves 4

6 tbsp vegetable oil or ghee

Whole garam masala (1 large Indian bay leaf, 1 piece cassia bark, 5 cm/2 inches long, 2 green cardamom pods and 2 cloves – see page 14)

250 g/9 oz onions, thinly sliced into half moons

2 tsp salt

4 whole skinless chicken legs (thigh and drumstick) (approximately 1.5 kg/3 lb 5 oz)

½ tbsp garlic paste

1 tbsp fresh ginger paste

1 tbsp ground coriander

500 g/1 lb 2 oz/1¾ cups full-fat Turkish or Greek yogurt

3 green chillis

Juice of 1 lemon

2 tbsp granulated sugar

A handful of mint leaves, to garnish

In a frying pan or deep saucepan that has a lid, heat the oil or ghee over a medium–high heat. Add the whole garam masala to the hot oil and cook, stirring, for a few seconds until the aromas are released from the spices.

Continue to stir the spices to prevent them from burning and add the sliced onions together with a pinch of salt. (Salt speeds up the process of sweating the onions.) Lower the heat to medium and cook the onions until they are soft and translucent. Do not allow the onions to brown as this is a pale dish. Depending on the variety of onion and its moisture content, this should take 10–12 minutes.

Add the chicken legs to the softened onions in the pan. Increase the heat to high and add the garlic and ginger pastes together with the ground coriander.

To avoid any lumps in the sauce, stir the yogurt before adding it to the chicken in the pan. When the sauce comes to the boil, lower the heat, cover and simmer for 25 minutes.

After 25 minutes, remove the lid and turn the pieces of chicken around, then cook for a further 10 minutes. Add the green chillis and simmer for another 10 minutes.

Take the chicken off the heat, then add the lemon juice and sugar, followed by the mint leaves.

———

Chicken Rezala can also be made using skinless, boneless chicken thighs cut into pieces. If using chicken thighs, reduce the overall cooking time from 45 minutes to 35 minutes.

Keema Sua Pulao
Mince with dill pulao

Inspired by the dill pulao made by a friend's Armenian mother, the addition of this fresh herb lends an unusual flavour within Indian cookery. During the 1930s and 40s, there was a thriving Armenian community in Calcutta who enjoyed the patronage of the British, but after Independence it dwindled in size. Today, there are few Armenian families left in Calcutta. This dish can be made using any kind of mince – beef, lamb, chicken, and even soy. Minced meat cooks quickly so this is a great dish to prepare when you are short of time. The rice can be made in advance, then reheated in a low oven without any fear of the meat disintegrating.

Serves 6

For the keema

2 tbsp oil

2 green cardamom pods

1 piece cassia bark, 1 cm/½ inch long (see page 13)

2 small Indian bay leaves

25 g/1 oz onions, finely chopped

¼ tbsp garlic paste

½ tbsp fresh ginger paste

500 g/1 lb 2 oz/2½ cups minced (ground) meat (beef, lamb, chicken) or soy

¼ tsp chilli powder (optional)

For the dill pulao

300 g/10½ oz/1½ cups basmati rice

3 tbsp vegetable oil

2 green cardamom pods

2 whole cloves

1 piece cassia bark, 2.5 cm/1 inch long (see page 13)

1 large Indian bay leaf

1 small–medium white onion (approximately 100 g/3½ oz), sliced into thin rings

1 small bunch dill, leaves stripped and chopped

Wash the rice in several changes of cold running water until the water runs clear, then place in a bowl and soak for 30 minutes in fresh water.

To make the keema, in a non-stick pan, heat 2 tbsp oil over a medium–high heat. Add the cardamom pods, cassia bark and bay leaves to the pan. Immediately add the onions and cook for 1 minute, stirring. Add the garlic and ginger pastes and cook for a further 1 minute.

Add the mince to the pan, breaking up any clumps with the back of a spoon. Add salt to taste. If using chilli powder, add this to the mince. Cook uncovered until all the liquid has evaporated from the mince. Avoid adding any water, but if the mince sticks to the base of the pan, add a splash of water. Once cooked, remove from the heat and set aside.

To make the pulao, in a heavy-based pan that has a lid, heat the oil over a medium–high heat. Add the onion rings and fry until caramelized. Using a slotted spoon, remove the onions and place on a plate to drain. Spread the onions across the plate so they crisp as they cool. Add the cardamom pods, cloves, cassia bark and bay leaf to the pan. After a few seconds, remove from the pan with a slotted spoon and set aside.

Put the kettle on to boil. Add the rice to the pan and stir for 1 minute to coat in the spice-infused oil. Cover with 600 ml/1 pint/2½ cups boiling water from the kettle. Add ½ tsp salt and the cooked mince to the pan. Cook uncovered over a medium–high heat until the water has been absorbed by the rice (about 4 minutes). Cover with the lid, lower the heat and simmer for a further 15–20 minutes. Once cooked, remove the pan from the heat and, using a fork, gently mix the rice and add the dill. Cover and leave for a few minutes before serving with the onions.

Chukander Raita

Beetroot Raita V

This raita has the most gorgeous bubblegum pink colour. If you want to avoid getting sprays of bright pink beetroot juice all over your kitchen worktop and your clothes, you can always use a food processor to grate the beetroot instead of doing it by hand, which can be a messy affair. Rather than using thick Turkish or Greek yogurt, you can use low-fat or bio yogurt, but as the beetroot juices thin the yogurt, this will result in a runnier raita.

Serves 8–10

½ tsp cumin seeds

3 large beetroots (beets), uncooked

1 kg/2 lb 4 oz/3½ cups Turkish or Greek yogurt (10% fat)

¼ tsp chilli powder (optional)

¼ tsp sugar, or to taste (depending on the sweetness of the beetroots/beets)

1 level tsp salt, or to taste

In a heavy-based frying pan (skillet), dry roast the cumin seeds over a low heat until the seeds darken and release a nutty fragrance. Grind the roasted cumin seeds in a spice grinder or crush them with a pestle and mortar.

Peel the beetroot and grate into a large bowl.

In a separate bowl, beat the yogurt with a wooden spoon or balloon whisk until smooth. Add the ground cumin and chilli powder, then mix to combine. Add sugar and salt to taste.

Add the spiced yogurt to the grated beetroot and mix until the beetroot is coated in yogurt.

Before serving, taste to check the seasoning and adjust as necessary.

———

You can make this raita the day before and chill in the refrigerator until ready to serve.

Dahi Baingan
Spiced aubergine in garlic raita v

A great side dish to have with kababs and parathas, I love this combination of thinly fried aubergine slices covered in garlic raita. In fact, this is my all-time favourite raita. In my family, this garlicky yogurt was always considered superior to the simple cucumber and tomato raita. But as Dahi Baingan was only made for important feasts, I got to enjoy its garlic raita accompaniment infrequently. Nowadays, I treat myself to this delicious dish far more often.

Serves 8

For the spiced aubergine (eggplant)

4 medium aubergines (eggplants), thinly sliced into discs

1 tsp ground turmeric

½ tsp chilli powder

1 tsp salt

Oil, for frying

For the garlic raita

500 g/1 lb 2 oz/¾ cup full-fat Turkish or Greek yogurt

6 garlic cloves, crushed

½ tsp chilli powder

1 tsp salt

¼ tsp brown sugar

For the tempering

10 fresh curry leaves

3 dried red chillis, broken in half

To make the garlic yogurt, mix all the ingredients together in a bowl. Taste to check the seasoning and adjust as necessary. Place in a serving dish.

To make the spiced aubergines, rub the ground turmeric, chilli powder and salt into the aubergine slices. Set aside for 20 minutes. When ready to cook, squeeze the aubergine slices to remove any excess water.

Ideally, use a deep-fat fryer or, if you haven't got one, use a heavy-based saucepan over a medium–high heat to heat the oil to 180°C/350°F. Test the temperature by putting a cube of bread in the oil – if it immediately starts to crisp up then the oil is ready. Working in batches, deep-fry the aubergine slices until golden brown. Using a slotted spoon, remove from the oil and drain on a plate.

Layer the deep-fried aubergine slices on top of the garlic yogurt in the serving dish.

To make the tempering, in a small frying pan (skillet), heat 2 tbsp of the oil used to fry the aubergines. Add the curry leaves and dried red chillis and cook, stirring, for 1 minute. Pour over the aubergine slices and yogurt. Serve immediately.

Begun Bhaja
Spicy fried aubergine slices v

In Bengal, thinly sliced aubergines are fried and added to simple meals of rice, dal and chutney. This is the go-to vegetable side dish for most home cooks as it requires minimum preparation and is quick to cook. During the annual festival of Durga Puja in Calcutta, the celebrations take place in our local community pandal, or marquee, where the bhog, or feast food, offered to all the visitors is always Khichree (see page 121), Tamatar Ki Chutney (see page 160) and a slice of Begun Bhaja. If every person gets just a single slice of aubergine, that is enough to make a Bengali happy!

Serves 6

3 fat aubergines (eggplants)

6 tbsp vegetable oil (or less if grilling or barbecuing)

A few fresh coriander (cilantro) sprigs, to garnish

For the marinade

1 tsp ground turmeric

1 tsp ground coriander

1 tsp chilli powder

3 tbsp lime juice

1½ tsp salt

Place all the ingredients for the marinade in a small bowl and mix into a smooth paste.

Slice the aubergines into 5-mm/¼-inch discs. (It is important to cut the aubergine slices to the same thickness so they cook evenly.)

Rub the marinade on both sides of the aubergine slices and leave on a tray, covered, for 1 hour. (Salting aubergines is very common in India; it draws out any excess water, making the aubergine less 'sponge like' so they don't soak up as much oil when frying.)

Heat the oil in a wide frying pan (skillet) on a low–medium heat. Leaving behind as much liquid as possible, transfer the aubergine slices from the tray to the frying pan. Fry in the hot oil on each side for 5 minutes. If the aubergine slices soak up the oil very quickly, you may need to add a bit more oil. Alternatively, brush each side of the aubergine slices with oil and cook under a grill (broiler) or on a barbecue.

The aubergine slices are ready when they have a golden brown soft centre and a crispy skin around the edges. Remove from the oil and drain on paper towels to absorb any excess oil.

Serve while warm, garnished with coriander leaves, with rice and dal.

Paneer Malai Korma
Indian cheese korma V

This is one of my favourite ways to cook paneer. It needs very few ingredients and is quick to make, so this is the perfect dish for when you have guests. Paneer is now available in most supermarkets in the specialist Indian section; you can buy it either ready-cut in cubes or in a block and you can cut it yourself. However, paneer is extremely simple to make at home – I have perfected my recipe for this cheese over the years, which I am now sharing with you (see page 30). Serve this dish with rice or bread. If the latter, add a touch more hot water to the sauce so there is plenty to dunk the bread into.

Serves 6

6 tbsp vegetable oil (not olive oil)

4 medium onions, thinly sliced

2 tbsp garlic paste

2 tbsp fresh ginger paste

2 tsp ground coriander

1 tsp red chilli powder (adjust to taste)

4 tbsp tomato purée (tomato paste)

2 tsp salt

½ tsp sugar

1 kg/2 lb 4 oz paneer, home-made (see page 30) or ready-made, broken or cut into 5-cm x 2.5-cm/2-inch x 1-inch pieces

2 x 400-ml/14-fl oz tins full-fat coconut milk

2 tbsp ground almonds

To garnish

A handful of flaked almonds (optional)

A few sprigs of coriander (cilantro) leaves (optional)

In a heavy-based pan that has a lid, heat the oil over a medium–high heat. Add the onions and cook, stirring, until they start to colour. Continue stirring to prevent the onions from burning and sticking to the base of the pan.

Once the onions have started to brown, add the garlic and ginger pastes. After 1 minute, add the ground coriander and chilli powder. Cook, stirring, until the 'raw' smell of the pastes and spices has disappeared – usually under 1 minute. If the mixture sticks to the base of the pan, add a splash of water.

Add 125 ml/4 fl oz/½ cup warm water, followed by the tomato purée, salt and sugar. Increase the heat, bring the liquid to the boil, then reduce the heat. Cover with the lid and leave to simmer until the liquid has reduced and the oil has come to the surface.

Add the paneer to the pan and cook for 2–3 minutes. Then add the coconut milk along with the ground almonds and cook uncovered for a further 2–3 minutes.

If you make this dish in advance, reheat over a low heat but do not stir too much as the paneer may break up.

Before serving, garnish with flaked almonds and coriander leaves, if preferred.

Shahi Kofta
Lamb meatballs in a rich gravy

The word 'kofta' is derived from the Persian 'koftan', which is the grinding of meat to make into balls. Nowadays vegetarian koftas are made using plantains, marrow and paneer, so the term no longer refers exclusively to a meat dish but to any ingredient ground and then squeezed together to form a shape. Again, confusingly, that shape need not be round, but oval or anything inbetween! The one thing all kofta dishes do have in common is gravy. Without gravy, it is a kabab.

Serves 4

For the kofta

1 slice white bread

500 g/1 lb 2 oz minced (ground) lamb

1 medium egg

1 small white onion, finely chopped

4 green chillis, chopped

1 clove, ground to a powder

¼ tsp roasted ground cassia bark

½ tsp chopped green raisins (optional)

½ tsp chopped cashew nut (optional)

3 tbsp chopped coriander (cilantro) leaves

Vegetable oil, for deep frying

For the gravy

5 tbsp ghee or vegetable oil

2 dried red chillis, broken into half

Whole garam masala (2 cloves, 1 Indian bay leaf, 2 green cardamom pods – see page 14)

3 medium onions, chopped

1 tbsp garlic paste

1 tbsp fresh ginger paste

3 tsp ground coriander

¼ tsp ground turmeric

2 tbsp tomato purée (tomato paste)

2 tbsp ground almonds

To make the kofta, in a shallow dish, put the slice of bread in water. Remove the bread from the dish and squeeze out the water. Break the soaked bread into small pieces in a bowl. Add all the other kofta ingredients, except the oil, and mix together. Season with 1 tsp salt. Take a handful of the kofta mixture and roll into a golf-ball size ball (4 cm/ 1½ inches in diameter). Following the instructions below, test-fry one kofta, then adjust the seasoning before rolling the remaining mixture. If the kofta breaks up in the oil while test-frying, soak an extra half slice of bread and crumble this into the kofta mixture to bind it together.

Ideally, use a deep-fat fryer or, if you haven't got one, a heavy-based pan over a medium–high heat, to heat the oil to 170°C/350°F. Test the temperature by dropping a cube of bread into the oil – if it immediately crisps up then the oil is ready. Working in batches, deep-fry 5 or 6 koftas at a time until golden brown. Do not cook the kofta too quickly; if you do, the meatball will be raw inside. Using a slotted spoon, remove to a plate to drain and set aside.

To make the gravy, in a small pan, heat the ghee or oil over a medium heat. Add the dried red chillis and garam masala to the pan, followed by the chopped onions and garlic and ginger pastes. Fry gently until the onions turn golden brown. Add the ground coriander and turmeric to the pan and cook for 30 seconds. Add 2 tbsp water to prevent the onions sticking to the base of the pan. Lower the heat, then add the tomato purée. Cook, stirring, until the 'raw' smell of the pastes and spices has disappeared – usually less than 1 minute. Cook until the oil has separated from the mixture, then add 500 ml/17 fl oz/2 cups water, followed by the ground almonds, and cook for a further 2–3 minutes.

Add the koftas to the pan and simmer, gently, uncovered, in the gravy for a further 8–10 minutes, turning them very carefully a few times.

Kari Patta Ka Kaddu
Butternut squash with curry leaves V

While I have recommended butternut squash, this recipe works just as well with many autumnal vegetables and can be substituted by any other kind of squash, turnips, even parsnips, or if you can find it, the Indian pumpkin 'kaddu'. The quantity of vegetables needed depends on what else is being serving alongside: a good estimate is 150 g/5½ oz (peeled weight) per person for a side dish as part of a multi-course meal and 200 g/7 oz per person for a main or as the sole side dish.

Serves 5–6

1 kg/2 lb 4 oz (peeled weight) butternut squash (or autumn vegetable of your choice), peeled

½ tsp ground turmeric

1½ tsp salt

1 tsp cumin seeds

5 tbsp vegetable oil

1 tsp black mustard seeds

10 fresh curry leaves

3 dried red chillis

4 garlic cloves, sliced into slivers

A good pinch of sugar

Cut the peeled butternut squash (or your chosen vegetables) into 2.5-cm/1-inch cubes. Rub the turmeric and salt into the diced squash and set aside for at least 30 minutes.

In a heavy-based frying pan (skillet), dry roast the cumin seeds over a low heat until the seeds darken and release a nutty fragrance. Grind the roast cumin seeds in a spice grinder or crush them with a pestle and mortar.

When ready to cook, heat the oil in a deep saucepan that has a lid over a medium–high heat. Once the oil is hot, take the pan off the heat, wait for 1 minute and then add the mustard seeds, curry leaves, dried red chillis and garlic.

Return the pan to a medium heat and add the squash. The water content in the squash should add sufficient moisture, but if the mixture sticks to the pan, add a splash of water. Increase the heat to high and cook the squash, stirring to prevent them sticking, for at least 5 minutes to seal them in the hot oil and prevent them from disintegrating. When the squash is coloured on all sides, cover the pan with a lid, reduce the heat to low and cook until the squash is tender. Take a piece of squash from the pan to check that it is cooked through.

Add the sugar and the roasted and ground cumin and continue to cook, covered, over a low heat until the sugar has dissolved and the squash is infused with the spices. If there is any water left in the pan, remove the lid, increase the heat to high and cook, stirring gently, until evaporated.

Before serving, taste to check the seasoning and adjust as necessary.

Mattar Pulao
Rice with peas <u>v</u>

My reaction when I first saw a bag of frozen peas after moving to England was one of total disbelief. In India, peas were only available in winter and Mattar Pulao was essentially a winter rice dish. Before a feast or party, all the children in the house would be rounded up to pop the pea pods to make the pulao. I left India in 1991, when it was a very different world from the India of today. Satellite television had only just arrived and programmes offered Indians their first glimpse of Western food and cooking. The first time I saw my husband pour peas from a bag into a pan I was so surprised... I was imagining an army of children popping pea pods to fill those bags!

Serves 6

300 g/10½ oz/1½ cups basmati rice

3 tbsp vegetable oil

2 whole cardamom pods

1 piece cassia bark, 2.5 cm/1 inch long (see page 13)

2 whole cloves

1 large Indian bay leaf

1 small–medium white onion (approximately 100 g/3½ oz unpeeled weight), sliced evenly into rings

1 heaped tsp salt

100 g/3½ oz/¾ cup frozen peas, defrosted

Wash the basmati rice in several changes of cold running water until the water runs clear, then place in a bowl and soak for 2 hours in more fresh cold water. (If you do not have time to soak the rice for 2 hours, then do soak it for as long as possible before cooking – even the briefest soaking time makes a difference.)

When ready to cook, drain the soaked basmati rice and set aside. In a heavy-based pan that has a lid, heat the oil over a medium–high heat. When the oil is hot, add the cardamom pods, cassia bark, cloves and bay leaf to the pan. After a few seconds, when the spices begin to sizzle and pop, using a slotted spoon, remove them from the pan to a plate and set aside.

Using the same oil the spices were fried in, add the onion to the pan and fry gently, stirring occasionally, until golden brown and caramelized (see page 11). Using a slotted spoon, remove the onion from the pan and place on a plate to drain. Spread the onions across the plate so they crisp as they cool.

Put the kettle on to boil. Add the soaked, drained basmati rice to the pan. Stir for 1 minute to coat the rice in the spice mixture, then cover the rice with 600 ml/1 pint/2½ cups boiling water from the kettle.

Return the fried whole spices and caramelized onion rings to the pan in the rice water. Add the salt. Cook, uncovered, over a medium–high heat until the water has been almost absorbed by the rice (about 4 minutes). Once most of the water has absorbed, cover the pan with a lid, lower the heat and simmer for a further 5 minutes. Once the rice is cooked, add the peas and gently mix using a fork to lift and separate the grains. Cover again and leave for a further 5 minutes before serving.

Hyderabadi Tamatar Ka Cutt
Eggs in tomato gravy V

This wonderfully tangy, spicy gravy was a signature dish of my great-aunt, Farzana Monem. In 1955, she married my maternal grandfather's younger brother and moved to Calcutta to live with the extended family. Coming from a very distinguished family from Hyderabad, Farzana introduced my maternal family to a new kind of cuisine. Farzana did not cook from written recipes, but this is the recipe I have written after talking with her and experimenting in my London kitchen.

The tomato base to this gravy was always made with fresh tomatoes, which were slow-cooked and sieved. By using fresh tomatoes, the end result was always a bit watery, so the gravy was thickened with gram or chickpea flour. I discovered convenience of passata in 1997, when a friend invited me over for a pasta meal. The ready availability of sieved tomatoes takes away a lot of the labour from this most traditional Hyderabadi dish, which I hope you will make often.

Serves 6

1 large bunch coriander (cilantro), with roots, stalks and leaves

1.5 kg/3 lb 5 oz passata (strained tomatoes) (if you have slightly more due to the size of the box or bottle, add it all and then adjust the seasoning)

4 tbsp coriander seeds

2 tsp cumin seeds

40 fresh curry leaves

10 dried red chillis, broken in half

9 garlic cloves

1 piece fresh ginger, 5 cm/2 inches long

2 tbsp tomato purée (tomato paste)

2 tsp sugar

1 tbsp salt

4 tbsp vegetable oil

½ tsp nigella (black onion) seeds

5 medium eggs, hard-boiled, shelled and thickly sliced

Wash the coriander to remove any grit. If you cannot find a bunch with roots, then pick one with long stalks as this is where the flavour lies.

Pour the passata into a deep pan. During the cooking process, the tomato liquid will spit and splutter. Using a deeper pan will save having to wipe clean the hob (stove) and walls. Add the washed coriander stalks, coriander seeds, cumin seeds, 20 of the curry leaves and 4 of the dried red chillis to the passata in the pan. Chop 7 of the garlic cloves and all of the ginger into chunks, then add to the pan.

Place the pan over a medium–high heat and then, once the passata is boiling, lower the heat to maintain a steady low boil. Cook for 30 minutes. Allow to cool slightly before straining the passata into a bowl. Discard the contents of the sieve, then return the passata to the pan. Add 1 tbsp of the tomato purée to the pan along with the sugar and salt, then stir.

In a small frying pan (skillet), heat the oil over a medium–high heat. Slice the remaining garlic cloves into thin slivers. Working quickly so the tempering does not burn, add the garlic, nigella seeds, remaining curry leaves and dried chillis to the pan. Cook for a few seconds, then pour the tempering oil and spices over the tomato gravy.

Taste to check the seasoning and adjust as necessary. To serve, ladle the gravy into serving bowls and lay the egg slices on top.

Baingan Bharta
Puréed aubergine V

Similar in texture to the Middle Eastern dish baba ganoush, this smoky aubergine purée is a great accompaniment to almost any meal. Baingan Bharta also makes delicious canapés when spread on top of slices of bread or strips of pitta.

Serves 6

2 large aubergines (eggplants), (approximately 1 kg/2 lb 4 oz)

4 tbsp vegetable oil

150 g/5½ oz onions, diced

30 g/1 oz fresh ginger, bashed and finely chopped

150 g/5½ oz tomatoes, diced

4 green chillis

1 tsp chilli powder

1 tsp salt (adjust to taste)

A few sprigs of mint, to garnish

The aubergines can be prepared in either of two ways, roasted in the oven or charred directly over a gas burner.

If cooking in an oven, preheat the oven to 200°C/400°F/Gas Mark 6. Place the aubergines in an oven tray and roast for 25–35 minutes or until the skin is charred all over and the flesh cooked all the way through.

If cooking over a flame, using tongs, hold each aubergine directly over the burner of a gas hob (stove) until the skin is charred all over and the flesh cooked all the way through. (While this method gives the aubergines a wonderful smokiness, it can also be messy and you will need to clean all surfaces afterwards. For easier cleaning, line your hob with foil to catch any drips, then discard the foil after cooking.)

Once the aubergine is cool enough to handle, remove the skin and mash the flesh into pulp. Do not discard any juices as they add to the flavour.

In a small frying pan (skillet), heat the oil over a medium heat. Add the diced onions and chopped ginger and cook until softened and starting to colour.

Increase the heat to high and add the tomatoes and whole green chillis to the pan. Cook for 5 minutes or until the tomato mixture has reduced.

Add the mashed aubergine to the pan along with the chilli powder and salt. Keeping the heat on high, reduce the mixture to a thick paste.

Before serving, taste to check the seasoning and adjust as necessary.

To serve, garnish with sprigs of mint.

Channa Masala
Spiced chickpeas V

Chickpeas are hugely versatile. As a cheap and healthy source of protein, they often form part of an Indian family meal. If you are short on time, you can use tinned chickpeas, but rehydrated dried chickpeas give a much better result, so save the tinned ones for emergencies only.

Serves 6–8

450 g/1 lb/2²/₃ cups dried chickpeas (garbanzo beans) or 2 x 400-g/14-oz tins

1 tsp bicarbonate of soda (baking soda)

2 tbsp cumin seeds

60 g/2¼ oz anardana (dried pomegranate) seeds (or 2 tbsp lemon juice)

2 tsp chilli powder

2 tsp salt

200 ml/7 fl oz vegetable oil

100 g/3½ oz onions, thinly sliced

100 g/3½ oz grated fresh ginger

6 green chillis, cut into 2.5-cm/1-inch pieces

3 tsp amchur (dried mango) powder (or 2 tbsp tomato purée/paste)

1 tsp ground garam masala (see page 14)

To garnish

Lemon slices

Onion rings

Wash the chickpeas in cold running water, then place in a large pan that has a lid and soak overnight in 3 litres/4 quarts fresh cold water and the bicarbonate of soda.

When ready to cook, top up with another 500 ml/17 fl oz/2 cups cold water, place the pan over a high heat, bring the water to the boil, then cover with a lid. Simmer the chickpeas for 30–40 minutes, or until soft.

In a heavy-based frying pan (skillet), dry roast the cumin seeds and anardana seeds over a low heat until the seeds darken and release a nutty fragrance. Allow the roasted seeds to cool and then grind in a spice grinder or crush them with a pestle and mortar to a fine powder. Add this powder, along with the chilli powder and salt, to the cooked, drained chickpeas and stir well.

In a frying pan (skillet), heat the oil over a low heat and fry the sliced onions, grated ginger and green chilli pieces. Cook, stirring, for 10 minutes or until brown. Add the contents of the frying pan to the pan containing the chickpeas and stir well.

Add the amchur powder (or tomato purée) to the chickpeas, followed by the garam masala.

Finally, add 1 litre/1¾ pints/4 cups warm water and increase the heat to high. Cook for 20 minutes, or until any excess liquid has evaporated.

Before serving, taste to check the seasoning and adjust as necessary. (I often add a pinch of sugar.) Garnish with the lemon slices and raw onion rings.

Mattar Paneer
Peas with Indian cheese v

This is a dish my family would always order when we went out to eat in India. Paneer was only made in our home kitchen for large family gatherings and ready-made paneer was not available nearby. Unlike Saag Paneer, where the cheese goes into the spinach without being fried, in Mattar Paneer it is better to fry the cheese before adding to the thick tomato gravy with peas. Ordinarily, I do not garnish this dish as I love its contrasting colours and textures, but, of course, you are welcome to scatter over a few chopped coriander leaves.

Serves 6–8

175 ml/6 fl oz/¾ cup vegetable oil

500 g/1 lb 2 oz paneer, home-made (see page 30) or ready-made, cut into 2.5-cm/1-inch cubes

2 tsp cumin seeds

4 dried red chillis

1 large onion, finely chopped

4 garlic cloves, crushed

1 tsp ground turmeric

2 tsp salt

300 g/10 oz/2¼ cups frozen peas, defrosted

3 tbsp tomato purée (tomato paste)

500 ml/17 fl oz/2 cups warm water

A pinch of sugar

1 tsp ground garam masala (see page 14)

In a non-stick saucepan, heat the oil over a medium–high heat. Add the paneer cubes to the pan in a single layer. Cook, turning the cubes around quickly, to seal on all sides. Using a slotted spoon, remove the paneer cubes from the pan, then place on a plate and set aside.

Using the remaining oil, add the cumin seeds and dried red chillis to the pan, followed by the chopped onions and crushed garlic. Cook, stirring, for 5 minutes. Next, add the ground turmeric and the salt, stir for few seconds and then add the thawed peas.

Place the tomato purée in a small bowl, then add a small amount of the warm water and mix to make into a paste. Add the thinned-down tomato purée to the pan and continue to cook over a medium–high heat. Gradually add more of the warm water and cook, stirring, for 5–10 minutes until the gravy reaches the consistency of single cream.

Return the fried paneer cubes to the pan and stir gently to combine. Add a pinch of sugar.

Before serving, taste to check the seasoning and adjust as necessary.

To serve, sprinkle the ground garam masala over the Mattar Paneer and mix through.

Footprints along the riverbank

My passion for history was encouraged by my father, who was a master storyteller. He could recreate the atmosphere of great battles, bringing historical characters to life. In the early 1980s, Calcutta was plagued by long power cuts and sometimes there was no electricity for an entire evening. On these nights, we would gather by candlelight to hear my father recount the most amazing historical tales; in the flickering shadows, we would be transported to another era. Thanks to my father's storytelling through those long nights of darkness, I have a library of knowledge in my head, even though I have never read the travel stories of Ibn Battuta, *Plutarch's Lives* or *The Rommel Papers*. 'Look for the historical footprints, wherever you go,' my father told me. 'The men and women who came before you each left their mark. You need to look for them. This is how you can make sense of the world around you.'

The footprints that are most vivid in my memory are those in the thick silt along the Hooghly River, which flowed through the city of Calcutta and under the imposing Howrah Bridge. Calcutta has been the confluence of many cultures, from the Persians to the British, all of whom left their legacy on our culinary traditions. Today, Calcutta has a rich food heritage and for this we need to thank all those who came before us. As a child I remember sitting on the banks of the river and watching the tide coming in. The water slowly covered the silt banks exposed by the low tide. Any footprints along the riverbank were erased, until the next day when another traveller along the river would leave their mark on the damp silt.

Historically, the Hooghly River has been the route by which traders entered Bengal and, for many, it was their gateway to India. One person who has left their historical footprints along the riverbank is Job Charnock. In 2003, the Calcutta High Court declared that Job Charnock's name, as the founder of Calcutta, should be expunged from all records. (During my school years in Calcutta, he was still acknowledged as the founder of the city.) The East India Company had begun trading in Bengal after obtaining permission from the Mogul Emperor Shah Jahan, and the company established their first factory along the banks of the River Hooghly in 1640. Half a century after the original firman (royal decree) granting them trading rights in Bengal, the East India Company was forced out of Hooghly and Job Charnock, who was in charge of the company in Bengal, established a fortified factory and merged three villages close to Fort William into a single administrative area, calling it Calcutta.

The culinary traditions of the British are often disregarded by Indians, but there would be no Aloo Gobi in India if the British travellers had not introduced cauliflower in the early nineteenth century. I have included two Anglo-Indian recipes (pages 106 and 108) – as well as an Armenian dill pulao (page 68) and Persian-inspired dishes like the Rezala (page 66) and Sheermal (page 117) – to pay homage to those who travelled to the city of my birth, made it their home, and left behind a culinary legacy.

Shorshe Maach
Bengali fish in mustard sauce

Fish with mustard is a quintessential Bengali combination. Traditionally Bengal mustard seeds and fresh green chillis were ground to a paste with a splash of water over a stone grinder called a sil nora. My childhood memories are of waking up to the rhythmic sound of stone rocking on stone from the kitchen as the masala for the day was prepared in the traditional way. In the absence of a stone grinder, please feel free to use a food processor. This is not a dish for the faint-hearted as the mustard and green chilli flavour packs a punch.

Serves 6

800 g/1 lb 12 oz skinless and boneless cod
   or halibut fillets
1½ tsp salt
1 tsp ground turmeric
2 tbsp black mustard seeds
3 green chillis
4 tbsp vegetable oil or mustard oil
½ tbsp ground coriander
½ tsp ground cumin
½ tsp chilli powder
400 ml/14 fl oz/1½ cup warm water

To garnish
Whole green chillis
Coriander (cilantro) leaves, chopped

Cut the fish fillets into 6 equal portions. Mix ½ tsp of the salt and ½ tsp of the ground turmeric, then rub on all sides of the fish and set aside for 30 minutes.

Using a food processor, blitz the mustard seeds and green chillis to a thick, smooth paste.

In a shallow saucepan, heat the oil over a medium–high heat. If you are using mustard oil, heat the oil until it is smoking hot – this removes the bitter pungency of the oil – then bring it down to a medium–high heat. Add the fish to the pan and fry to seal each piece, but do not let them cook. Remove from the pan to a plate and set aside.

Lower the heat to medium, then add the mustard and chilli paste to the pan and cook for 1 minute. Next, add the ground coriander, ground cumin, chilli powder, and the remaining ½ tsp ground turmeric and 1 tsp salt and cook for a further 1 minute. Gradually add the warm water and cook, stirring, until the mustard and chilli paste and spices have amalgamated. Increase the heat to medium–high and reduce the liquid until the oil rises to the surface and seeps to the sides of the pan.

Carefully return the fish fillets to the pan, cover with the gravy and cook evenly on both sides – this should take no more than 6 minutes.

Before serving, taste to check the seasoning and adjust as necessary.

To serve, garnish with the whole green chillis and chopped coriander.

Bihari Saag
Spinach with garlic <u>v</u>

Spinach is a seasonal vegetable in India and, during its short season in Calcutta, we would eat a spinach dish almost daily. The queen of Indian spinach dishes is Sarson Da Saag, which combines mustard greens with spinach. As it is difficult to source mustard greens outside India, I have made this recipe a simple spinach dish. If you have access to interesting varieties of spinach leaves and greens, add them to this recipe and experiment with flavours and textures.

Serves 6

4 tbsp ghee

4 dried red chillis, broken in half

6 garlic cloves, crushed

1 kg/2 lb 4 oz/20 cups fresh spinach leaves or mixed green leaves

½ tsp salt (adjust to taste)

In a large pan, heat the ghee over a medium–high heat. Add the dried red chillis, followed by the garlic. Add the spinach leaves and salt, then cook until the spinach has wilted and any excess liquid released by the spinach has evaporated.

Before serving, taste to check the seasoning and adjust as necessary.

————

Although the spinach leaves will reduce dramatically in volume during the cooking process, always use a large pan in which the fresh spinach leaves fit.

Attae Ka Paratha
Wholemeal bread v

The dough of this paratha needs to rest before you can roll it out. Rolling out perfect circles can sometimes be a challenge, especially if you are entertaining family and friends and do not want to waste a lot of time. This paratha square can be made in advance and rolled out at the last minute.

Makes 8

450 g/1 lb/3½ cups wholemeal (whole wheat) or chapati flour

1 tsp salt

300 ml/10 fl oz/1¼ cups water

50 g/2 oz/4 tbsp butter or ghee, melted (or use oil)

Vegetable oil, for cooking

To make the dough in a food processor, place the flour and salt into the bowl. Using the paddle attachment, gradually add the water to the bowl. Do this very slowly so you do not end up with a sticky mess.

To make the dough by hand, place the flour and salt into a large bowl. Gradually add the water, working the dough until it is smooth, elastic and no longer sticky.

On a lightly floured work surface, knead the dough for at least 5 minutes. Place in a lightly floured bowl, cover, and leave to rest for 30 minutes.

Once rested, divide the dough into eight equal pieces.

Roll out each piece of dough to a 30-cm/12-inch disc. To shape the paratha, fold the top third of the disc down into the centre. Brush the dough with the melted ghee or butter, then lightly dust with flour. Next, fold the bottom third of the disc up into the centre. Again, brush with melted ghee or butter, then dust with flour. Now, turn the folded paratha 90 degrees clockwise and fold the top third down into the centre. Brush with more melted ghee or butter and dust with flour. Lastly, fold the bottom third up into the centre to make a square. Repeat with all pieces of dough. Keep each square separate so they do not stick to each other, cover with a clean dish towel and set aside until you are ready to cook.

When ready to cook, roll out each paratha to a 3-mm/⅛-inch thick square.

Put a tawa (flat iron griddle pan) or a non-stick frying pan (skillet) over a medium heat. Cooking one paratha at a time, drizzle oil around the edges of the pan and, using paper towels, press the paratha down in the pan to ensure it cooks evenly. Turn the paratha over and cook the other side in the same way. The bread is cooked when it is freckled with small brown patches on both sides.

Dum Gosht
Spicy beef roast

When raising children in a different country from the one where you were born, you discover interesting things as they grow older. For one, your children will speak with an accent different from yours. Also, if you are South Asian, your children will be less adept at eating rice with their hands. My kids found eating meat on the bone a real fiddle – probably because they did not use their hands to get all the meat out. So this is a compromise dish: a very Western-style joint of meat but cooked using traditional Indian spices.

Serves 8

4 dried red chillis, broken in half

1 tbsp desiccated coconut

1 tbsp poppy seeds

1 tsp cumin seeds

½ tsp coriander seeds

6 tbsp ghee

2 medium onions, chopped

200 g/7 oz/1 cup natural (plain) yogurt

2 tbsp garlic paste

2 tbsp fresh ginger paste

1 tbsp fennel seeds

1½ tbsp salt

1.5 kg/3 lb 5 oz topside of beef, trimmed of all fat

In a dry frying pan (skillet), roast the dried red chillis, coconut, poppy, cumin and coriander seeds until they darken and release their aromas. Immediately remove the pan from the heat, pour the contents onto a cool plate and spread them out so they do not continue to cook. Once the spices have cooled, grind them to a fine powder and set aside.

In a deep pan, heat the ghee over a medium–high heat. Add the onions and fry until golden brown and caramelized (see page 11). Remove to a plate to drain. Set aside the ghee to use later. Grind the onions to a paste.

Place the yogurt in a bowl and mix in the ground onions with the garlic and ginger pastes, the toasted spice mixture, fennel seeds and salt. Stir until the ingredients are evenly combined. Using the tip of a sharp knife, make deep slashes in the beef. Work the yogurt into the beef, making sure all surfaces are covered. Leave to marinate for 2 hours in the refrigerator, or even longer if possible. Before cooking, take the beef out of the refrigerator to allow it to return to room temperature.

The beef can be roasted in the oven or cooked on the hob (stove). If roasting, preheat the oven to 200°C/400°F/Gas Mark 6. In a roasting tray or pan, heat the ghee in which the onions were fried. Add the beef and seal the joint until brown all over. If oven-roasting, place the beef in the preheated oven. Check on the beef during the cooking time to make sure it is roasting evenly. Roast for 1 hour for medium-rare. For well-done, cook for a further 10–15 minutes. If cooking in a pan, add 500 ml/17 fl oz/ 2 cups warm water to the pan and cook over a medium heat until the beef is cooked to your liking. If there is any liquid left in the pan once the meat is ready, increase the heat to high and evaporate the liquid.

As soon as you take the beef joint out of the pan or oven, cover it with foil and leave to rest for 10 minutes before slicing.

Unday Ka Halwa
Egg halwa <u>V</u>

This halwa is an unusual dessert in the Indian sub-continent as it is not made using the usual flour, nuts or vegetables. In some royal households, halwa is sometimes made with a very unusual ingredient – meat! In our family, this halwa was made only on very special occasions when we had a distinguished visitor. As with all recipes using eggs, buy the best-quality eggs you can afford and use them as soon as possible while they are fresh.

Serves 6–8

1.5 litres/2½ pints/6 cups plus 4 tbsp whole milk
10 strands good-quality saffron
8 large eggs
450 g/1 lb/2¼ cups granulated sugar
200 g/7 oz/1¾ sticks unsalted butter
Almonds and pistachio slivers, to garnish

Gently warm 4 tbsp of the milk in a pan. Do not boil the milk; it should only be tepid as you do not want to scald the saffron. Touch the surface of the milk to check the temperature, then add the saffron strands and leave to infuse.

Beat the eggs and sugar together in a bowl. Melt the butter in a heavy-based pan on a low heat. It is important to keep the heat low during the entire cooking process to prevent the eggs from hardening and ending up like sweet scrambled eggs.

Slowly incorporate the egg and sugar mixture into the melted butter, followed by the rest of the milk (not the saffron infused milk as yet).

This halwa needs to be cooked for over 45 minutes on a very low heat. Keep stirring to prevent the egg mixture from getting burnt at the bottom. After 20 minutes add the saffron-infused milk and saffron and keep stirring. The halwa is ready when the eggs take on a grainy texture and the ghee is separating from the mixture.

Serve the halwa at room temperature, garnish with the almond and pistachio slivers.

Boora Chenni Ki Kheer
Rice pudding with brown sugar V

A version of this dessert is made in almost every Indian household. Many years ago, when I did not have enough white sugar to make the kheer, I replaced it with brown sugar. I was absolutely delighted with the result, which resembles the Bengali jaggery kheer I ate as a child. You can use any kind of brown sugar for this recipe, but I prefer using a dark unrefined sugar. The sugar measurement is a rough estimate as the sweetness will vary depending on the type of sugar used. Adjust the sweetness to your taste, but remember that the kheer will taste less sweet once it cools. The ideal container to cool and serve this dessert in is an unglazed terracotta bowl. It adds a beautiful earthiness and flavour to the dish. Of course, you can use any other serving dish or pour the kheer into individual bowls.

Serves 6–8

30 g/1 oz/2 tbsp basmati rice

2.4 litres/80 fl oz/10 cups whole milk

4 green cardamom pods

1 large Indian bay leaf

4 heaped tbsp brown sugar (adjust depending on the type of sugar used)

Pistachio slivers, to garnish (optional)

Wash the rice in several changes of cold running water until the water runs clear, then place in a bowl and soak for 30 minutes in fresh water.

In a heavy-based pan, heat the milk over a medium–high heat, stirring frequently, until it comes to a boil. Once boiling, add the cardamom pods and bay leaf, keeping it on a low, rolling boil for 45 minutes.

Drain the soaked rice and add to the milk. The rice may stick to the base of the pan, so stir more frequently once the rice has been added. Cook for a further 15 minutes, or until the milk has reduced by half. Add the sugar to the rice mixture and stir gently until it has dissolved. Taste to check the sweetness, but remember that the kheer will taste less sweet once it cools.

Remove the pan from the heat and allow the kheer to cool for 1 hour, then transfer to a container, cover, and place in the refrigerator for 2 hours.

When ready to serve, ladle the kheer into bowls and garnish with pistachio slivers.

Feasting with Friends

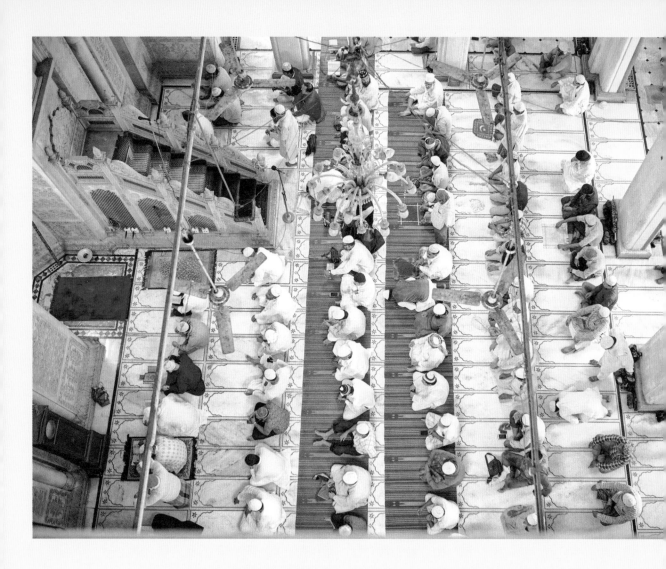

Mughlai food

Mughlai food is the style of cuisine linked to the medieval Mughal Empire. The early Mughal rulers came to India from Central Asia and brought with them their Turkish and Mongol culinary heritage. The second influence on Mughlai cuisine was Persia. The second Mughal ruler, Humayun, lost his throne in 1540 and then he and his court spent 15 years in exile to Persia where they had diplomatic ties to the Safavid rulers. In food-speak, diplomatic ties can be interpreted as the Mughal nobility feasting at the Persian courts, where the Mughal entourage were entertained as honoured guests.

Farsi was the court language when Humayun returned to rule in India. The large number of Persians who returned with Humayun may have been the reason why there was a shift in culinary dominance at the royal court from Turkish to Persian cuisine. The third Mughal ruler, Akbar, was born in India and it was under his rule that the local Indian traditions merged with Central Asian, Persian and Turkish cultures, most visibly in Mughal architecture but also in Mughal kitchens.

The Mughlai influence on my cooking is linked to my family heritage. While my parents came from different regions of India with distinct culinary traditions, Mughlai spicing and cooking techniques were common to both their cuisines. Bengal has its own style of cooking, much of it based around fresh fish and mustard. The Mughlai cuisine of Bengal is very different; linked to the Muslim population living there, it originated from the port where traders from Central Asia, Persia and the Middle East had settled. The Murgh Rezala (see page 66) and Chicken Chaap (see page 136) recipes are two distinct dishes which hail from Bengal. My father's family home was geographically close to the royal courts of Delhi and Awadh, and many of the dishes like the Yakhni Pulao (see page 138) are speciality Mughlai dishes from that region.

Words like 'Shahi', which means royal, and 'Mughlai' are often over- and inaccurately used in many Indian restaurants to describe a dish. I have recipes in this book that have Mughal roots and, once you make them, I hope you will be able to recognize the distinct style of this cuisine. The food is light and fragrant, the spicing is layered, and doesn't simply rely on spices like turmeric and cumin.

Zafran Murgh Korma
Saffron chicken korma

There are many ways to cook a korma. If you ever get the chance to try a Safed Korma from Hyderabad, grab it. The pale, almost bland, appearance is deceptive. The name Safed Korma, which means white, hides a fragrant and delicately spiced dish. For a dish to be called a korma it usually has to be meat, although it can sometimes be vegetable-based, and braised in a yogurt base. Used sparingly in Indian kitchens due to it being an expensive spice, the addition of saffron gives this dish a lovely colour and also makes it very special.

Serves 4 as a main course or 8 a part of a multi-course meal

500 g/1 lb 2 oz/1¾ cups Turkish or Greek yogurt (10% fat)

1 tbsp garlic paste

2 tbsp fresh ginger paste

8 medium skinless chicken thighs (on the bone) (approximately 1 kg/2 lb 4 oz)

2 tbsp whole milk

A large pinch of good-quality saffron strands

6 tbsp vegetable oil

3 medium white onions, evenly and thinly sliced into rings

Whole garam masala (2 Indian bay leaves, 1 piece cassia bark, 2.5 cm/1 inch long, 3 green cardamom pods and 1 clove – see page 14)

1 tbsp ground coriander

¼ tsp chilli powder

1 tsp salt

2 tbsp ground almonds

1 tbsp sugar

A small handful of almond flakes, to garnish

In a small bowl, combine the yogurt with the garlic and ginger pastes. Place the chicken thighs in a non-reactive container with a lid and spoon over the marinade, making sure that every surface of the chicken is covered. Cover the container and place in the refrigerator for 30 minutes.

Gently warm the milk in a pan. Do not boil the milk; it should only be tepid as you do not want to scald the saffron. Touch the surface of the milk to check the temperature, then when the milk is tepid add the saffron strands and leave to infuse.

In a deep pan or wok that has a lid, heat the vegetable oil over a medium–high heat. Add the onions to the pan and fry gently, stirring occasionally, until golden brown and caramelized (see page 11). Using a slotted spoon, remove the onions from the pan, leaving as much of the oil in the pan as possible to cook the other ingredients, and place on a plate to drain. Spread the onion rings across the plate so they crisp as they cool.

Add the whole garam masala to the same pan and oil used to fry the onions. After a few seconds, add the ground coriander and continue to cook, stirring. After 1 minute, add the marinated chicken to the pan along with the marinade from the container. Keeping the heat on medium–high, continue stirring gently. After 5 minutes, or when the oil separates from the yogurt and comes to the surface, add the chilli powder and salt. Lower the heat, cover the pan with the lid and simmer gently for 35 minutes. The chicken is ready when the edges have softened and are slightly curled.

Remove the pan from the heat. Add the saffron-infused milk, ground almonds and sugar. Stir the softened chicken gently to avoid breaking it up.

Before serving, taste to check the seasoning and adjust as necessary. Garnish with the flaked almonds and the fried onions.

Aloo Dum
Spicy potatoes V

A brief note about spices. Panchporan is a spice mix used in eastern India from Bengal, Assam, and Orissa all the way up to the foothills of the Himalayas. It is a mixture of five seed spices: mustard seeds, cumin seeds, nigella seeds, fennel seeds and fenugreek seeds. While it is perfectly easy to make at home, panchporan is available in most Indian spice shops, online, and in some larger supermarkets.

One seed spice in panchporan worth mentioning is fenugreek. Cultivated by the Assyrians around 3,000 years ago, fenugreek is considered by ancient Ayurvedic traditions to contain beneficial properties, helping to lower blood sugar and stimulate the production of insulin. As part of the five-seed spice mix, the bitterness of fenugreek is balanced by the flavours of the other four spices.

Serves 6–8

1 kg/2 lb 4 oz potatoes (any variety, though ordinary white waxy potatoes work best), unpeeled

1½ tsp salt

6 garlic cloves, ground to a paste

2 tbsp tomato purée (tomato paste)

½ tsp chilli powder

2 tbsp vegetable, sunflower or groundnut oil

½ tsp panchporan (see page 14)

A handful of coriander (cilantro) leaves, picked or chopped, to garnish

Place the potatoes in a large pan that has a lid and fill with water. Add 1 tsp of the salt. Place the pan over a high heat and bring to the boil. The cooking time for the potatoes will vary according to their variety, size and quality.

While the potatoes are cooking, in a small bowl, mix together the garlic paste, tomato purée, chilli powder and the remaining ½ tsp salt. Set aside.

Test the potatoes to check that they are cooked. Using the point of a sharp knife or skewer, pierce the middle of the largest potato. The potatoes should be tender but not falling apart. Once the potatoes are cooked, drain them in a colander and leave to cool. When they are cool enough to handle, remove the skins from the potatoes, then cut them into 2.5-cm/1-inch cubes and set aside.

Heat the oil in a large pan over a medium heat. Add the panchporan to the pan. Wait for the spice seeds to pop before adding the garlic, tomato and chilli mixture. Cook, stirring, for a few minutes until the oil separates and the mixture has darkened.

Add the diced potatoes to the pan and coat them well with the garlic, tomato and spice mixture. Turn the heat to low, cover the pan and cook for 5 minutes.

To serve, garnish with coriander leaves.

Anglo-Indian Coconut Rice v

Most Indians would not associate Bengal with coconut rice as it is more common to use coconut in South Indian and some western Indian rice dishes. However, this rice dish, cooked in coconut milk, is popular among the Anglo-Indian community in Calcutta. I add some water along with the coconut milk, but you can use all coconut milk, if you prefer.

Serves 6

300 g/10½ oz/1½ cups basmati rice

3 tbsp vegetable oil

1 small white onion (approximately 100 g/ 3½ oz), evenly and thinly sliced into half moons

4 green cardamom pods

4 cloves

1 piece cassia bark, 2.5 cm/1 inch long (see page 13)

1 large Indian bay leaf

¼ tsp ground turmeric

1 tsp salt

1 x 400-ml/14-fl oz tin coconut milk

200 ml/7 fl oz/¾ cup warm water

Wash the basmati rice in several changes of cold running water until the water runs clear, then place in a bowl and soak for 30 minutes in more fresh cold water.

In a heavy-based frying pan (skillet), heat the oil over a medium–high heat. Add the sliced onions to the pan and fry gently, stirring occasionally, until golden brown and caramelized (see page 11). Using a slotted spoon, remove the fried onions from the pan, leaving as much of the oil in the pan as possible to cook the other ingredients, and place on a plate to drain. Spread the onions across the plate so they crisp as they cool.

Drain the soaked rice and then spread it on paper towels to remove as much excess water as possible.

Put the pan with the oil back over a medium–high heat. Add the cardamom pods, cloves, cassia bark, bay leaf and ground turmeric in quick succession, followed by half the caramelized onions and the rice. Stir to coat the rice with the spice-infused oil. Add the salt, followed by the coconut milk and water. (If you prefer to use all coconut milk, add 600 ml/20 fl oz/2½ cups.)

Bring the contents of the pan back to the boil, then lower the heat, cover the pan and leave to simmer. After 15 minutes, check to see whether all the liquid has been absorbed by the rice. If there is any liquid left in the pan, replace the lid, then check again after 5 minutes.

To serve, garnish the rice with the remaining caramelized onions.

Anglo-Indian Ball Curry

Certain dishes made in Calcutta by the Anglo-Indian community bear a similarity to other dishes. This meatball curry looks like a classic kofta dish, but has something distinctive about it – the inclusion of parsley. My friend's mother grew parsley especially for this dish, even though it was not a herb commonly used by the locals. I presume this was a legacy of the memsahibs of the Raj, who probably grew parsley in their gardens. The Anglo-Indians also had a great love affair with coconut. I use thick coconut cream in this recipe. The meat used in this curry was almost always beef. The meatballs are not fried before being added to the gravy, instead they are cooked directly in it. As long as you roll the meatballs tightly and do not stir the contents of the pan too much, they should not break up in the gravy.

Serves 8

For the meatballs

1 kg/2 lb 4 oz/4½ cups finely minced (ground) beef

2 tbsp finely chopped parsley

3 green chillis, finely chopped

1 tsp salt

For the gravy

4 tbsp vegetable oil

3 onions, ground to a paste

1 tbsp garlic paste

2 tbsp fresh ginger paste

1 tbsp ground coriander

¼ tsp chilli powder

1 tsp salt

2 tbsp tomato purée (tomato paste)

500 ml/17 fl oz/2 cups thick coconut milk

1 tsp ground garam masala (see page 14)

A handful of parsley leaves, chopped (optional)

To make the gravy, in a deep saucepan, heat the oil over a medium–high heat. Add the ground onions and fry for 4–5 minutes. Add the garlic and ginger pastes to the pan and cook for a further 5 minutes. If the contents are sticking to the base of the pan, add a splash of water.

Add the ground coriander, chilli powder and salt to the pan, then cook, stirring, for 2 minutes.

Add 500 ml/17 fl oz/2 cups water to the pan, increase the heat to high and bring to a boil. Add the tomato purée, then stir until the gravy is smooth. Lower the heat to low, then prepare the meatballs.

To make the meatballs, place all the ingredients in a bowl, mix together and knead gently. Divide the mixture and make 20 golf-ball-sized meatballs, 4 cm/1½ inches in diameter. Roll each meatball between your hands to make sure there are no open cracks or seams, which will make the ball break up in the gravy.

Once the meatballs are made, increase the heat under the gravy pan to medium. Add the meatballs one at a time. Shake the pan to roll the balls in the gravy. Do not use a spoon to turn the meatballs as they may break. Continue to cook, uncovered, over a low–medium heat for 20–30 minutes. Add the coconut milk to the pan and cook, stirring, for a further 5 minutes.

Before serving, taste to check the seasoning and adjust as necessary. (The only accurate way to assess the seasoning is to taste a meatball with the gravy. I prefer not to season this dish.) To serve, sprinkle the ground garam masala over the curry and mix through. If preferred, garnish with more chopped parsley leaves.

Newari Salad
Himalayan spicy potato salad V

An unusual recipe from the region, this is a cold potato salad. The Nepali community on both sides of the border make this 'Aloo Achaar', as they call it. For North Indians, achaar means pickle. Apart from the chillis, there is nothing pickle-like in this dish. This salad tastes even better the next day, so it should be your go-to salad if you are preparing for a big celebration feast or barbecue. A word of warning: this potato salad is very spicy. The addition of fenugreek seeds to the tempering gives this dish a unique flavour; a bitter seed used frequently in India to regulate and lower blood sugar and stimulate the pancreas to produce more insulin.

Serves 10

1 kg/2 lb 4 oz waxy potatoes (or new potatoes)

2 tsp salt

1 whole cucumber, cut into long strips using a peeler, to garnish

For the dressing

100 g/3½ oz/¾ cup sesame seeds

4–6 dried red chillis

8 tbsp sesame oil

6 tbsp lemon juice

For the tempering

2 tbsp vegetable oil

12 fenugreek seeds

Place the potatoes in a large pan that has a lid and fill with water. Add the salt. Place the pan over a high heat and bring to the boil. The cooking time for the potatoes will vary according to their variety, size and quality.

While the potatoes are cooking, make the dressing, in a dry frying pan (skillet), roast the sesame seeds with the dried red chillis until the chillis turn a couple of shades darker. Remove from the heat immediately and spread on a plate to cool. When cool enough to handle, using a pestle and mortar, grind the sesame seeds and chillis to a powder. In a large bowl, mix the sesame oil with the lemon juice, then add the ground sesame seeds and chilli to the oil mixture.

Test the potatoes to check that they are cooked. Using the point of a sharp knife or skewer, pierce the middle of the largest potato. The potatoes should be tender but not falling apart. Once the potatoes are cooked, drain them in a colander and leave to cool. When they are cool enough to handle, remove the skins from the potatoes, then cut them into 2-cm/¾-inch cubes and set aside.

Place the diced potatoes in the bowl with the dressing. Toss until all the potatoes are well coated in the dressing.

The final stage is the tempering. In a small frying pan (skillet), heat the oil over a high heat. Working quickly so the tempering does not burn, add the fenugreek seeds. The moment the seeds start to pop, pour the tempering oil and spices over the potato salad. Mix well.

Taste to check the seasoning and adjust as necessary; you may want to add more lemon juice. To serve, garnish with long strips of cucumber.

Channa Dal
Split yellow channa lentils <u>V</u>

If you cannot find channa dal in your local store, you can substitute yellow split peas. Although toor dal or yellow split pigeon peas look similar, they are quite different from channa dal, which is a yellow split chickpea. Channa dal takes longer to cook than masoor or mung dal and requires pre-soaking before cooking. The added time needed to cook this dal is well worth the effort though, making a thicker, richer and more nutritious lentil dish. The important final stage is the tempering, or 'baghar' as they call it in my tradition.

Serves 8

For the dal
500 g/1 lb 2 oz/2¾ cups channa dal
2 tbsp garlic paste
1 tsp ground turmeric
2 tsp chilli powder
2 tsp salt

For the tempering
6 tbsp ghee or vegetable oil
2 dried red chillis
1 tsp cumin seeds
1 medium onion, thinly sliced into half moons

To garnish
Green chillis, chopped
Coriander (cilantro) leaves, chopped
Fresh ginger, cut into slivers

Wash the channa dal in cold running water, then place in a large pan and soak for at least 4 hours in more fresh cold water.

When ready to cook, transfer the soaked, drained channa dal to a heavy-based pan that has a lid and cover with 8 cm/3 inches of water. Add the garlic paste, ground turmeric, chilli powder and salt, then bring to a boil over a medium–high heat. Once the channa dal is boiling, lower the heat, cover the pan and simmer for 40 minutes. Regularly remove any scum that floats to the surface of the water. Check whether the dal is soft by using the back of a wooden spoon to 'break' the lentils. Be careful not to mush the dal; the aim is to break down some of the lentils to thicken the dal. If it looks too dry, add a splash of warm water. When ready, the dal should have the consistency of a thick, textured soup.

Before serving, taste to check the seasoning and adjust as necessary. Once the dal is ready, place it in a bowl and keep warm while preparing the tempering.

In a small frying pan (skillet), heat the ghee or oil over a high heat. Working quickly so the tempering does not burn, add the dried red chillis, cumin seeds and sliced onions. Cook until the onions are golden brown and caramelized (see page 11). Pour the tempering oil and spices over the warm dal and stir gently. Next, take a spoonful of the dal and place it in the frying pan to absorb any remaining oil – take care whilst doing this as the oil may splutter. Tip the spoonful of dal back into the main dal bowl.

To serve, garnish the dal with the chillis, coriander and ginger slivers.

Tamatar Raita
Tomato raita <u>v</u>

I prefer my raitas thick, so I usually use full-fat Turkish yogurt that has already been hung and drained. You can also use natural or plain yogurt, but make sure it is full-fat as low-fat varieties are not a good option. You can make this raita in advance and keep it in the refrigerator. However, a word of warning: the chillis will infuse into the yogurt and – depending on when you add them – they can make the raita spicy. For a mild raita, add the green chillis just before serving. If you want a spicy raita, by all means mix in the chillis earlier, but either way chop the chilli pieces large enough for your guests to see in case they want to avoid eating them.

Serves 8–10

1 tbsp cumin seeds

1 kg/2 lb 4 oz/3½ cups full-fat Turkish or Greek yogurt

1 tsp salt (adjust to taste)

4 large tomatoes, finely diced

1 medium red onion, finely diced

2–3 green chillis, cut into 1-cm/½-inch pieces

½ tsp brown sugar

A handful of mint leaves, to garnish

Place a dry frying pan (skillet) over a medium–high heat. Add the cumin seeds and roast them until they darken and release their aromas. Remove from the heat and then, using a pestle and mortar, grind the cumin seeds to a powder.

In a small bowl, mix all the ingredients together.

Taste to check the seasoning and adjust as necessary.

To serve, garnish with fresh mint leaves.

Kaju Aloo
Potatoes with cashew nuts V

Dosas are a South Indian speciality, a thin crêpe made from a lentil and rice batter filled most commonly with a stuffing made from potatoes. However, my dosa-making skills are poor – I always fail to achieve the thin crisp crêpe that is the hallmark of a good dosa – so I console myself by making Kaju Aloo, the potato stuffing of my favourite masala dosa. The combination of mustard seeds, curry leaves and cashew nuts works really well in this dish. A word of advice: if you are using super-spicy green chillis in this recipe, you may want to reduce the quantity you use by a bit.

Serves 6

1 kg/2 lb 4 oz large standard white potatoes (such as Maris Piper), unpeeled

6 green chillis

1 piece fresh ginger, 4 cm/1½ inches long

2 tbsp vegetable oil

1 tsp black mustard seeds

12 fresh curry leaves

1 tbsp cashew nuts

2 large onions, cut into small chunks

1 tsp ground turmeric

1 tsp salt

½ tsp sugar

Place the unpeeled potatoes in a large pan that has a lid and fill with water. Place the pan over a medium–high heat and bring to the boil. Lower the heat to low–medium and keep on a low rolling boil for 20–25 minutes. The cooking time for the potatoes will vary according to their variety, size and quality. Test the potatoes to check that they are cooked. Using the point of a sharp knife or skewer, pierce the middle of the largest potato. The potatoes should be tender but not falling apart. Once the potatoes are cooked, drain them in a colander and leave to cool. When they are cool enough to handle, remove the skins from the potatoes, then cut them into 2.5-cm/1-inch cubes and set aside.

Using a food processor, blitz the green chillis and ginger together to make a paste. If you want to reduce the heat of this dish, remove the chilli seeds.

In a frying pan (skillet) with a lid, heat the oil over a medium–high heat. Add the mustard seeds to the pan followed by the curry leaves and cashew nuts and cook until the cashew nuts darken in colour. Next, add the onions and cook until soft, translucent but not coloured.

Add the chilli and ginger paste to the pan along with the ground turmeric, salt and 200 ml/7 fl oz/1 cup water, bring to the boil, cover, and simmer for 10 minutes. Remove the lid and add the diced potato. Bring the mixture back to the boil, then lower the heat, add the sugar and cook, covered, for a further 10 minutes. If there is any excess water in the pan, remove the lid and cook over a high heat until the potatoes have a glossy sheen.

Before serving, taste to check the seasoning and adjust with more salt or sugar as necessary.

Puri
Deep-fried bread V

Puris are perfect when entertaining; needing less time-consuming preparation than parathas, these puffed round breads are an impressive addition to any feast table. The dough for the puris can be prepared and rolled before guests arrive, then fried as the other dishes are being served. If you are making puris for a large gathering, using a food processor makes the preparation easier. To make more puris, multiply the quantities given, but the resting time for the dough remains the same.

Makes 8

225 g/8 oz/1¾ cups plain (all-purpose) flour (not strong bread flour)

½ tsp salt

2 tbsp melted ghee, butter or vegetable oil

150 ml/5 fl oz/²/₃ cup warm water

500 ml/17 fl oz/2 cups vegetable oil, for deep frying

Sift the flour and salt into a large bowl. Add the melted ghee, butter or oil and rub into the flour until it is thoroughly incorporated.

Gradually add the warm water in dribbles until the dough is pliable but quite stiff. Depending on the flour used, you may not need all the water.

Turn the dough out onto a lightly floured work surface and knead for 4–6 minutes until smooth and silky. Cover the dough with a clean dish towel and leave to rest for 1 hour. You can prepare the dough the day before and leave it in an airtight container in the refrigerator, then take it out 1 hour before rolling out the dough to bring it to room temperature.

When ready to cook the puri, roll out the dough into a long rope approximately 20 cm/8 inches long. Divide the rope into eight equal portions. Roll each portion into a ball and then, using a rolling pin, flatten into a 13-cm/5-inch disc that is 3 mm/¹/₈ inch thick. Once rolled, place each flattened puri disc on a plate and cover with a damp cloth while you roll out the remaining puris.

To fry the puri, ideally use a deep-fat fryer or, if you haven't got one, a heavy-based saucepan, karai or wok over a medium–high to heat the oil to 190°C/375°F. Test the oil temperature by putting a cube of bread in the oil – if it immediately starts to crisp up then the oil is ready. Working one at a time, slide a puri disc sideways into the hot oil to ensure it reaches the bottom of the pan without folding over. Within seconds the disc will bob to the surface of the oil.

There are two ways to make a puri puff up. For the first, using the back of a slotted spoon, push the puri down into the hot oil. For the second, spoon hot oil from the pan over the surface of the puri. Once it puffs up, turn the puri over and leave it for a few seconds before removing from the oil. Place on paper towels to drain. Serve immediately while hot.

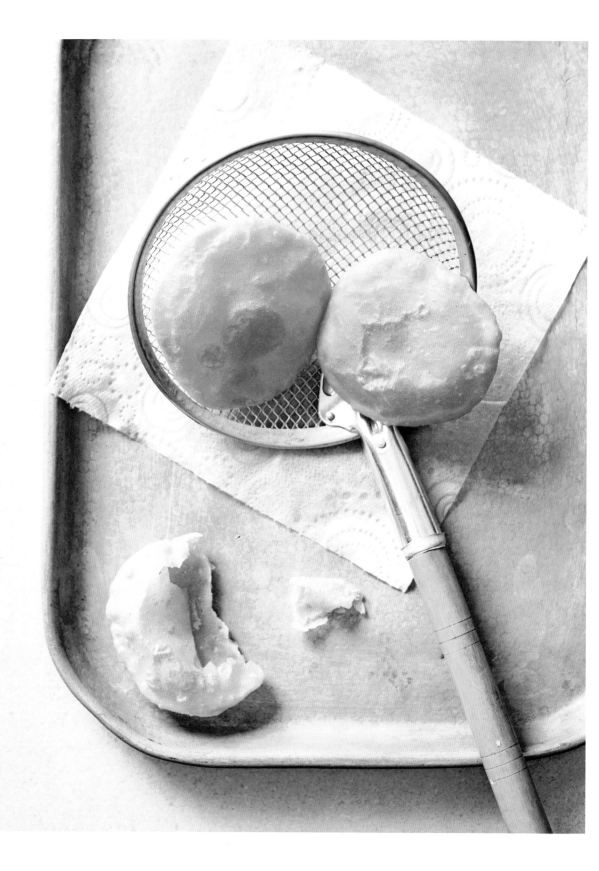

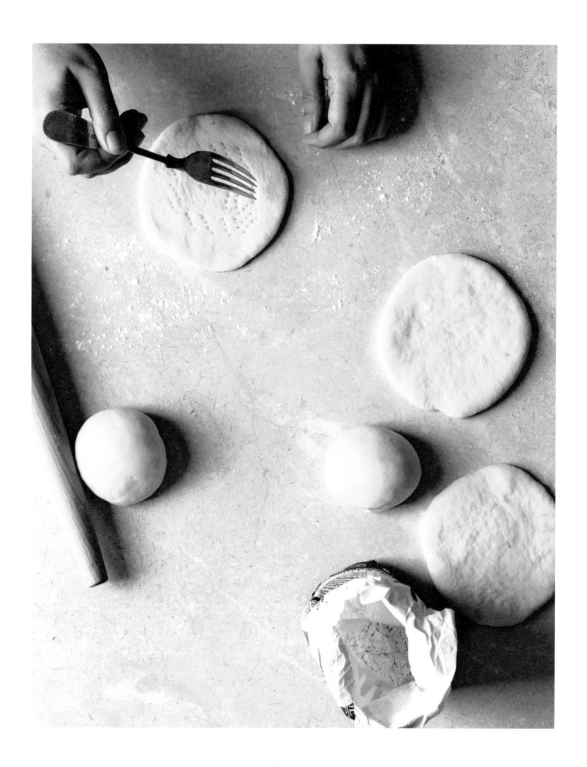

Sheermal
Baked saffron bread v

A Persian-inspired baked bread, sheermal is usually served on special occasions and at Mughlai weddings. This is a good bread to make when entertaining as it can be made in advance and kept warm. It can also be reheated at the last moment in a toaster. As every toaster is different, it is worth testing the setting before your guests arrive to make sure the bread is heated through and you do not burn the sheermal – or set off your fire alarm. The infusion of the saffron strands in the milk is an important necessary step, so make sure you allow at least an hour for this stage.

Makes 6

150 ml/5 fl oz/²/₃ cup whole milk

10 strands good-quality saffron

330 g/11½ oz/scant 2½ cups plain (all-purpose) flour (not strong white bread flour)

½ tsp salt

2 tsp dried instant yeast

1 tbsp sugar

2 medium eggs, beaten

50 g/1¾ oz/3½ tbsp melted unsalted butter or ghee, plus an extra 1 tbsp for brushing

Gently warm 50 ml/2 fl oz/¼ cup of the milk in a pan. Do not boil the milk; it should only be tepid as you do not want to scald the saffron. Touch the surface of the milk to check the temperature, then add the saffron strands and leave to infuse for 1 hour.

When you are ready to make the dough, in another pan, gently warm the remaining milk. Sift the flour into a large mixing bowl and add the salt, yeast and sugar. Make a well in the centre of flour and pour in the beaten eggs and milk. Mix all the ingredients together with your hands until they come together to form a soft dough, adding half of the infused saffron milk in the final stages of bringing the dough together. Cover the dough with a clean tea towel and set aside for 1 hour.

Before rolling out the sheermal, preheat the oven to 200°C/400°F/Gas Mark 6.

Divide the dough into 6 equal pieces. Roll out each piece into a 15-cm/ 6-inch disc, 5 mm/¼ inch thick. Keeping the outside 2.5 cm/1 inch clear, prick the middle of the discs with a fork to prevent the sheermal from puffing up in the oven. Place the discs on a baking tray lined with parchment paper. Brush the top of each disc with the remaining milk and bake in the preheated oven for 10–12 minutes.

When the sheermal is ready, remove from the oven and brush the tops of each bread with the melted butter or ghee.

Sultans of the kitchen

During an interview, I was once asked to name a female icon who I looked up to. In that moment, the first person to come to mind was not a woman working in food but the first and only female ruler of Delhi. Razia Sultan ruled Delhi from November 1236 to October 1240. Razia was the daughter of Iltutmish, who began his life as a Turkish slave but became the Sultan of Delhi. Despite having male heirs, Iltutmish recognized the merit of his daughter and named her as his heir. On becoming Sultan, Razia faced constant hostility from Turkish nobility in the Delhi court for being a woman, with accusations of love affairs. Although acknowledged by her contemporaries as a just ruler and an able administrator, Razia was eventually removed from the throne by the all-male nobility group, and her brother made ruler.

The term Sultan is more commonly applied to male rulers, but the word derives from the arabic term 'sultah', meaning authority or power. I wonder if her story might have had a different ending if, during her reign as Sultan, Razia had gathered around her a group of like-minded supportive women, installed an all-female cabinet and made the commander of her army a female warrior. Our restaurant, Darjeeling Express in Kingly Court, London, is run by an all-women kitchen and, coincidentally, the entire team who worked on this cookbook were all female.

When I was shown a rough draft of the cover for this book, I was totally stunned. It reminded me so much of the portraits I have seen of Razia Sultan. My next thought was that, although it has my face, the portrait represents all the generations of nameless, faceless, silent South Asian women who cooked and fed their families. They were never acknowledged. They were never immortalized in portraits. Their contribution was taken for granted. To the women of my kitchen, and to the women of kitchens everywhere... We are the Sultans of the kitchen.

119

Machi Kabab
Fish balls with coconut and mint chutney

These monkfish kababs are great served as a canapé or finger food. For ease of eating, encourage your guests to pierce each ball with a toothpick before dipping them into the Coconut and Mint Chutney. Every region in India has a favourite chutney. Unlike in the West, where chutneys are mostly cooked, the chutneys served in India are freshly made and rarely contain oil. The cashew nuts give an interesting texture and thicker consistency, but they can be omitted if you prefer. To thin the chutney into more of a dipping sauce, add some yogurt. If you don't have time to make a chutney at all, a simple bowl of crème fraîche works really well with these kababs, too.

Serves 8

4 slices of white bread

1 kg/2 lb 4 oz monkfish tails

2 tsp lemon juice

1 tsp white pepper

1½ tsp salt

60 g/2¼ oz white onions, finely chopped

4 garlic cloves, finely chopped

4 green chillis, finely chopped

4 tbsp finely chopped coriander (cilantro) leaves

2 eggs, beaten

Vegetable oil, for deep frying

For the Coconut and Mint Chutney

3 green chillis

1 piece fresh ginger, 1 cm/½ inch long

2 tbsp lemon juice

1 tbsp brown sugar

1 tsp salt

100 g/4 oz fresh mint leaves, shredded

80 g/2¾ oz coconut, ideally fresh, grated

80 ml/2¾ fl oz/⅓ cup cold water

To make the chutney, place all the ingredients in a food processor and blend to a smooth paste. Alternatively, grind each ingredient separately using a pestle and mortar until smooth and mix together. Set aside.

To make the breadcrumbs, dry out (but do not toast) the slices of bread under a grill (broiler). Using your hands, crumble the bread into a small bowl, or use a food processor, and set aside.

In a colander set over a pan of boiling water, gently steam the monkfish tails for 5–6 minutes. Remove the fish from the colander, pat dry with paper towels, then flake the fish into a bowl.

To the same bowl, add the lemon juice, white pepper and salt. Combine. Then add the onion, garlic, chillis, coriander leaves and breadcrumbs and mix through. Finally, add the beaten egg and bring the mixture together.

Ideally, use a deep-fat fryer or, if you haven't got one, use a heavy-based saucepan over a medium–high heat to heat the oil to 190°C/375°F. Test the temperature by putting a cube of bread in the oil – if it immediately starts to crisp up then the oil is ready.

Take a handful of the fish mixture and roll it into a ball the size of a walnut. Carefully roll this kabab into the hot oil to 'test fry'. Cook for until golden brown. Using a slotted spoon, remove the kabab from the oil and allow to drain on paper towels. When cool enough to eat, check the kabab for seasoning. If necessary, adjust the seasoning of the fish mixture. Continue making the rest of the balls in the same way and frying them in small batches of 5 or 6. Serve immediately, while the kababs are hot, with the room-temperature chutney on the side.

Khichree
Spiced rice and lentils V

This is the dish to cook when friends are coming over, but your day has not gone to plan and you need to get dinner cooked in less time than planned. A classic comfort food, Khichree is a combination of rice and lentils that is – and was always – served at my home with big dollops of the iconic Indian butter, Amul.

Serves 6

300 g/10½ oz/1½ cups basmati or long-grain rice

150 g/5½ oz/scant 1 cup masoor dal (red lentils)

100 ml/3½ fl oz/²/₅ cup melted butter or ghee, or vegetable oil

½ tsp cumin seeds

6 whole black peppercorns

1 Indian bay leaf

1 green cardamom pod

2 cloves

1 piece cassia bark, 2.5 cm/1 inch long (see page 13)

1 piece fresh ginger, 2.5 cm/1 inch long

2 tsp salt

750 ml/25 fl oz/3¼ cups warm water

2 green chillis

Dollops of salted butter (optional, but highly recommended)

Wash the rice in several changes of cold running water until the water runs clear, then place in a bowl and soak for 30 minutes in more fresh cold water. Repeat for the lentils.

In a pan, heat the butter, ghee or oil over a medium–high heat. Add the cumin seeds followed immediately by the peppercorns, bay leaf, cardamom pod, cloves, cassia bark and ginger. Cook, stirring, for 2–3 minutes.

Add the soaked, drained lentils to the pan. Stir for 1 minute to coat the lentils in the spice mixture. Next, drain and add the rice and stir gently so as not to break up the grains. Add the salt and 750 ml/25 fl oz/3¼ cups warm water to cover the rice and lentils. Bring the pan to the boil and then cook, uncovered, over a medium–high heat for about 4 minutes, or until the water has been almost absorbed by the rice.

Add the fresh green chillis, then cover the pan with the lid, lower the heat and simmer for 20 minutes, or until the grains of rice are plump and the lentils are soft, but still whole and intact. After 20 minutes, check the rice and lentils – there should be no liquid at the edges of the pan – and gently run a fork through to lift and separate the grains. Replace the lid, remove from the heat and leave for a further 5 minutes to allow any remaining moisture to be absorbed.

Before serving, taste to check the seasoning and adjust as necessary. Serve immediately, while the khichree is hot, with dollops of salted butter dotted over the top.

Gobi Musallam
Spiced whole cauliflower V

I have adapted the classic Mughlai recipe, Murgh Musallam, to create this dish. Musallam means 'whole' and, in my family, we make this spiced whole cauliflower dish for special guests so it looks as visually impressive as any of the meat dishes on the table. Since my brother married a vegetarian, my mother has mastered the art of converting traditional heritage meat recipes into vegetarian dishes. This is one of them. Conveniently, this cauliflower dish can be prepared and cooked in advance, then reheated in a low oven.

Serves 4–6

1 tbsp whole milk

6 strands good-quality saffron

6 tbsp ghee

1 medium cauliflower, trimmed

2 medium onions, thinly sliced into half moons

1 tbsp garlic paste

2 tbsp fresh ginger paste

500 ml/17 fl oz/2 cups full-fat natural (plain) yogurt

1 tsp ground garam masala (cloves, cardamom, cassia bark, Indian bay leaf, nutmeg and mace roasted and ground – see page 14)

1 tbsp ground coriander

½ tsp chilli powder

1½ tsp salt (adjust to taste)

1 tsp sugar

4 drops of natural orange food colouring (optional)

Almond and pistachio slivers, to garnish

Gently warm the milk in a pan. Do not boil the milk; it should only be tepid as you do not want to scald the saffron. Touch the surface to check the temperature, then add the saffron strands and leave to infuse.

In a pan or wok, heat the ghee over a medium–high heat. Add the whole cauliflower and fry until brown on all sides. Remove from the pan, place on a plate to drain and set aside.

In the ghee left in the pan or wok, fry the onions until golden brown and caramelized (see page 11). Remove the onions to a plate to drain. Grind the onions to a paste.

Stir the onion, garlic and ginger pastes into the yogurt, then add the ground garam masala, ground coriander, chilli powder, salt, sugar, saffron-infused milk and food colouring (if using).

Place the whole cauliflower base down in a deep cast-iron casserole dish. Pour the yogurt marinade over the cauliflower, then cover loosely with parchment paper and leave for 20 minutes.

Place the casserole dish over a medium heat to cook the cauliflower, keeping it loosely covered with the parchment paper. Lift the paper and baste the cauliflower regularly with the yogurt sauce to make sure it cooks evenly – depending on the size of the cauliflower, this should take 30–40 minutes. The cauliflower is cooked when a skewer goes in easily with only a slight resistance. Do not overcook the cauliflower: bear in mind that the cauliflower will continue to cook a little after you take it off the heat.

Before serving, taste to check the seasoning and adjust as necessary. To serve, place the cauliflower whole on a serving plate or dish, then garnish with almond and pistachio slivers. Slice to serve.

Bharwa Simla Mirch
Stuffed bell peppers

In India, we call bell peppers 'capsicum', so I was surprised when, on my first solo shopping trip after moving to England, the vegetable seller in Cambridge Market Square gave me a blank look when I asked for capsicums. I pointed to what I wanted, then he told me, 'Love, they're called peppers.' This recipe can be adapted to suit vegetarian or meat-eating guests by stuffing the bell peppers with either Aloo Dum or Keema. If serving both, colour code them using green bell peppers for the vegetarian version and red bell peppers for the meat option to avoid any confusion. Select bell peppers that are the same size. This is not for aesthetic reasons; the peppers must cook at the same rate, so you do not want any to be over- or undercooked. This recipe is also a great way to use up leftovers.

Serves 4

For the bell peppers
4 medium bell peppers, all the same size
Salt
1 lemon, thinly sliced

For the filling options
1 quantity of Aloo Dum (see page 104)
or
1 quantity of Keema (see page 69)

Preheat the oven to a moderately high temperature of 190°C/375°F/ Gas Mark 5.

Wash the bell peppers. Using a sharp knife, slice the top off the bell peppers to make a lid, leaving the stalks in place. Set the lids aside.

Clean the inside of the bell peppers, removing the seeds and membranes. Lightly season the inside of the bell peppers and line the base with a thin slice of lemon.

Stuff the bell peppers with the filling of your choice. Add more thin slices of lemon on top of the filling, then replace the lids on top of the bell peppers.

Stand the stuffed bell peppers in an oiled roasting pan and cover with foil to prevent the tops from burning. Place in the preheated oven. After 30 minutes, check the bell peppers. They should now be browned on the outside and possibly wrinkled, but still be holding their shape. If they are not ready, return to the oven for a further 10 minutes, but try not to overcook them as they may collapse and soften.

To serve, garnish the bell peppers with the remaining lemon slices.

Shahi Tukra
Royal morsel V

This is a special Mughlai dessert, which is served at festive occasions and weddings across the Indian sub-continent. Originating from the Mughal palaces, the literal translation of 'Shahi Tukra' is 'Royal Morsel'. Soaked in saffron-and-cardamom-infused milk and garnished with slivers of pistachio and almond, in this recipe the humble slice of bread is transformed into a fragrant, delicate dessert. Surprisingly simple to make, Shahi Tukra is the Indian version of bread and butter pudding. It is a great way to end any meal, but it is particularly suitable for larger parties as it can be made in advance and served either at room temperature or chilled.

Serves 8

1 litre/34 fl oz/4 cups plus 4 tbsp whole milk

¼ tsp good-quality saffron strands

2 green cardamom pods

225 g/8 oz/1¼ cups granulated sugar

8 slices of white bread (one or two days old)

6 tbsp melted butter

6 tbsp sunflower oil

4 tbsp clotted (heavy) cream

1 tbsp almonds slivers, to garnish

1 tbsp pistachios slivers, to garnish

Gently warm 2 tbsp of the milk in a pan. Do not boil the milk; it should only be tepid as you do not want to scald the saffron. Touch the surface of the milk to check the temperature, then add the saffron strands and leave to infuse.

Pour the rest of the milk into a separate pan and add the cardamom pods. Over a medium–high heat, bring the milk to the boil. Add the sugar to the milk and stir gently until the sugar has dissolved. Lower the heat to low, then add the saffron-infused milk to the pan. Leave the milk pan on a low heat.

Cut the bread slices in half diagonally into triangles.

In a non-stick frying pan (skillet), warm the butter and oil over a medium heat. One piece at a time, add the bread to the pan and fry on both sides. When the bread turns brown, remove from the pan and immerse in the warm milk for no more than a 10–15 seconds. Once the bread has softened in the milk, remove with a slotted spoon and layer in a serving dish. Repeat for the remaining bread and continue layering the fried and soaked slices in the serving dish.

Once all the bread has been layered in the dish, pour the 150 ml/5 fl oz/²/₃ cup of the remaining warm milk over the slices. Cover the dessert and set aside; the bread will absorb some of the extra milk in the serving dish.

Before serving, either gently spread or dot the clotted cream over the top of the bread. This does not have to be in an even layer. Sprinkle slivers of almonds and pistachios across the top. Serve either at room temperature or chilled.

Nimbu Pani
Indian lemonade v

Nimbu Pani is the drink traditionally offered to visitors in Indian homes during the summer months. Sadly, this tradition is slowly dying out as more and more families have refrigerators and the preferred drink for many now is fizzy cola. This drink can be rustled up in no time at all, and the ingredients are easily available. The Himalayan rock salt can be left out, as not everyone likes its pungent sulphuric flavour, but do try this lemonade with the salt at least once – it works beautifully.

Serves 8

5 tbsp sugar (adjust to taste)

Juice of 6 lemons

A large pinch of Himalayan rock salt (optional)

Crushed ice

To garnish

A few fresh mint leaves

Slices of lemon

In a jug or pitcher, dissolve the sugar in the lemon juice. Add 1 litre/34 fl oz/4 cups cold water and a pinch of the rock salt, then stir to combine.

To serve, fill a glass with crushed ice and pour over the lemonade. Garnish with fresh mint leaves and a slice of lemon.

Burhani

Green chilli and mint yogurt drink v

In Bengal, burhani is usually served at Muslim weddings to accompany the classic rice dish, biryani. The biryani of Bengal is not super-spicy, so the contrast of this chilli and mint yogurt drink makes a great combination. You can reduce the heat of this drink by using green chillis that are slightly less fiery. (See page 129 for photograph.)

Serves 6

1 kg/35 oz/5 cups full-fat natural (plain) yogurt
2 green chillis
2 tbsp chopped mint leaves
1 tsp salt
¼ tsp sugar (adjust to taste)
½ tsp white peppercorns
1 tsp cumin seeds
1 tsp coriander seeds
¼ tsp yellow mustard seeds

To garnish
Green chillis
A few sprigs of mint

Using an electric whisk or balloon whisk, beat the yogurt until smooth.

Finely grind the chillis and fresh mint to a paste, then add to the beaten yogurt and stir to combine. Season with the salt and sugar.

In a dry frying pan (skillet), roast the peppercorns and other whole spice seeds until they darken and release their aromas. Transfer to a plate and leave to cool for 5 minutes before grinding in a spice grinder or pestle and mortar.

Add the ground spices to the yogurt and stir to combine. The salt will break down the yogurt, thinning it slightly, but if it is still too thick to drink, thin the yogurt down with 1 or 2 tbsp cold water.

Before serving, taste to check the seasoning and adjust as necessary.

To serve, cut a slit into the green chillis and slide one on to the rim of each glass,, then garnish with the mint leaves.

Gulab Lassi
Rose yogurt drink V

A floral lassi which works well for a large gathering of friends, such as at a barbecue. Using the best-quality rose essence is important as you want to have a good rose flavour in the lassi. I am usually not a big fan of adding artificial colour to food, but you might want to add a few drops of food-safe colouring to this yogurt drink.

Serves 12

2.4 litres/80 fl oz/10 cups full-fat natural (plain) yogurt

150 g/5 oz/¾ cup granulated sugar

4 tbsp rose essence

12 ice cubes

A few of drops of pink food-safe colouring (optional)

A handful of rose petals, to garnish (optional)

Blend the yogurt, sugar and rose essence in a blender or food processor until smooth.

Add the ice cubes and blend for a few moments more until the yogurt turns frothy.

If you are using food colouring, add a few drops of the pink food-safe colouring and blend again.

Pour into serving glasses, then scatter a few rose petals over the top of each glass, if preferred.

Celebratory Feasts

Dawaat دعوت

Dawaat is a feast, usually to celebrate something joyous. I feel fortunate to have grown up in a large close-knit family where food was at the heart of every celebration. I also feel fortunate to have grown up in the pre-tech age, which meant that nobody had mobile phones or personal computers, so conversation was the main form of entertainment. In my family we held frequent dawaats. With such a large family, someone was always getting married or having children or relatives were visiting. Entertaining visiting relatives was always the best dawaat, as the family put on a good show to impress.

The family feast was also a chance for my great-aunts to cook their speciality or signature dishes. We always looked forward to the feast at my great-aunt's house. Farzana Chachi would cook spectacular Hyderabadi food. Nobody in the family tried to copy her dishes or ask for her recipes as that would have been almost disrespectful. If anyone else were to replicate those dishes, it would have taken the shine off her family feasts. The dawaat was always served on large sharing platters. There were too many of us to sit around a dining table. Typically there would be a centrepiece dish – something grand and gorgeous – with plenty of other equally impressive side dishes. An average family dawaat would involve between seven and ten dishes.

Last year I visited Calcutta to bid goodbye to the ancestral family home where I spent my childhood and enjoyed endless feasts. The home has been sold and will be demolished to make way for a high-rise building. Rather than a visit of sadness, my aunts and mother decided to make my visit a celebration and hosted a beautiful feast for me on the veranda outside the rooms of my great-grandfather. Each great-aunt made one of her signature dishes. This was a very unusual feast as I cannot ever remember attending a collaborative feast before where each family cook made one dish. It was a journey of flavours and aromas – my childhood journey – and to make the day complete my brother, sister and cousin flew in to attend the dawaat. A poignant meal, yet a happy and fulfilling one. I left my ancestral home with memories of this last dawaat etched in my heart forever. Some of those family feasting dishes are in this chapter as I want to share the joy of cooking and serving a dawaat with you, reader.

Chicken Chaap

This is a unique dish from Bengal, a korma infused with mace and nutmeg that is quite different from the super-sweet, raisin-and-nut-filled kormas served in many restaurants. I avoid using food colouring in my recipes, preferring saffron, which means this korma will not have the bright orange colour usually associated with this dish. If you have a good-quality, food-safe colouring, you may use it if you prefer.

Serves 6

¼ tsp good-quality saffron strands or a few drops of orange food colouring

10 tbsp sunflower oil or other neutral oil

5 onions, thinly sliced into half moons

1.2 litres/40 fl oz/5 cups thick Turkish or Greek yogurt

2 tbsp chopped garlic

2 tbsp chopped fresh ginger

6 skinless, bone-in chicken thighs

1 tbsp ground coriander

2 tsp mild chilli powder (preferably Kashmiri)

4 tsp salt

4 tsp sugar

2 tsp flaked almonds, to garnish

For the garam masala

2 tsp cloves

4 black cardamom pods

1 nutmeg

2 large pieces mace

6 Indian bay leaves

To make the garam masala, in a dry frying pan (skillet), roast all the ingredients over a medium heat, stirring continuously to prevent them burning. The spices are ready when the cloves swell, turn grey, and pop. Allow the spices to cool, then grind to a fine powder in a spice or coffee grinder. Grate the nutmeg, before adding it to the spice grinder. Any unused garam masala can be kept in an airtight container for a few weeks.

If using saffron to colour the dish, in a small bowl, infuse the saffron strands in 4 tbsp tepid water.

In a frying pan (skillet), heat 6 tbsp of the oil over a medium–high heat. Add the sliced onions to the pan and fry gently, stirring occasionally, until golden brown and caramelized (see page 11). Using a slotted spoon, remove the onions from the oil, leaving as much of the oil in the pan as possible to use later, and place on a plate to drain. Spread the onions across the plate so they crisp as they cool.

In a large bowl, mix the yogurt with the garlic, ginger, 1 tbsp of the garam masala and the oil retained from the caramelized onions. If using orange food colouring, add this directly to the yogurt.

In a pan that has a lid, heat the remaining 4 tbsp oil over a medium–high heat. Add the chicken and seal on all sides. Lower the heat to medium and pour the yogurt mixture over the chicken. Keep the heat at medium so the contents of the pan do not boil. Add the caramelized onions and ground coriander and cook, stirring continuously, for 10 minutes.

When the oil rises to the surface and the yogurt splits, add the chilli powder and salt. Bring the sauce to a boil, then reduce the heat. Add the infused saffron at this point, if using. Cover and cook the chicken for a further 10 minutes. Add the sugar and stir to mix thoroughly.

Before serving, taste to check the seasoning and adjust as necessary. To serve, garnish with flaked almonds.

Yakhni Pulao
Rice cooked in chicken stock

The essence of this pulao is the yakhni, which means 'meat stock' or 'broth': the delicate flavour of the chicken stock is absorbed by the rice. Do use chicken thighs on the bone when preparing the stock, rather than boneless thighs or breasts, to ensure the stock has flavour. The name 'Yakhni' – and some of the spices – is Kashmiri, but this dish is not made in Kashmir. Rather, it hails from modern-day Uttar Pradesh. One theory regarding the origin of this pulao is that it was made in the palace of the ruler of Oudh – modern-day Lucknow – in the nineteenth century by Kashmiri cooks. The pale colour of this pulao is deceptive; it is packed with flavour and spices. This is a wonderful one-pot dish to make for the entire family. For feeding children, you may want to swap the fresh green chillis for a couple of mild chillis.

Serves 6

400 g/14 oz/2 cups basmati rice

Salt

3 tbsp oil

2 medium onions, finely sliced

1 kg/2 lb 4 oz skinless bone-in chicken thighs, cut in half

2 or 3 green chillis (optional)

A few sprigs of mint, to garnish (optional)

For the spice bag

6 garlic cloves, cut in half

1 piece fresh ginger, 5 cm/2 inches long, cut into thick slices

6 green cardamom pods

6 cloves

2 pieces cassia bark, each 2.5 cm/1 inch long (see page 13)

1 black cardamom pod

3 or 4 medium Indian bay leaves

2 heaped tbsp fennel seeds

2 tsp coriander seeds

Wash the rice in several changes of cold running water until the water runs clear, then place in a bowl and soak for 30 minutes in more fresh cold water with ½ tsp salt.

In a frying pan (skillet), heat the oil over a medium–high heat. Add the sliced onions to the pan and fry gently, stirring occasionally, until golden brown and caramelized (see page 11). Using a slotted spoon, remove the onions from the oil, leaving as much of the oil in the pan as possible to cook the chicken, and place on a plate to drain. Spread the onions across the plate so they crisp as they cool.

Keeping the heat on medium–high, add the chicken to the pan and seal it on all sides. Return half the caramelized onions to the pan.

To make the spice bag, place the spices in a piece of cheesecloth or muslin and knot the corners securely together so the bag does not open during cooking process.

Add the spice bag to the pan. Pour over enough cold water to cover the chicken and add 2¼ tsp salt. Bring the water to the boil, then lower the heat, cover with a lid and leave to cook for 20 minutes. After 10 minutes, check the chicken to make sure it is not falling apart.

Once the chicken is cooked, using a slotted spoon, carefully remove the chicken from the pan and place on a plate, trying to keep the meat on the bone.

For the yakhni, you will need approximately twice the volume of stock to rice (so 4 cups of stock to 2 cups of rice). If you have more than 4 cups, reduce the stock. If you have less than 4 cups, add some water.

Return the 4 cups of stock to the pan. Drain the rice and add to the pan, together with the chicken and green chillis, if using. Place the pan over a medium–high heat. Leaving the spice bag in the pan, bring the stock to the boil. Once boiling, lower the heat, cover with a lid and leave to simmer. Check the pan often to see if the stock has been absorbed, but that the rice still retains some bite, about 15–25 minutes.

At this point, remove the rice pan from the direct heat and reduce the heat to low. Place the rice pan on a tawa (flat iron griddle pan), or the closet thing you have to a tawa – an iron plate or a flat pan – to diffuse the heat. Leave the rice pan on the tawa over a low heat for 10 minutes. Alternatively, place the rice pan in a preheated low oven for 10 minutes.

Once the pan has been removed from the heat source, cover the top of the pan with a cdish towel and leave it undisturbed for 10 minutes.

Check the rice – there should be no liquid at the edges of the pan – and gently run a fork through to lift and separate the grains.

To serve, remove the spice bag and garnish with the remaining caramelized onions and sprigs of mint.

Zafrani Murgh
Saffron roast chicken with apricots

Not a lot of Indian food is cooked in an oven. When inviting friends and family over for a meal, this can sometimes present a challenge as often there are not enough hobs or burners in a home kitchen to cook and reheat all the dishes. This chicken recipe can be roasted in the oven and, if you time it correctly, it can be served immediately without needing to be reheated. In our tradition, we do not eat chicken skin and so I have used a skinned whole chicken here. You can leave the skin on if you prefer, but please do make sure the chicken is properly marinated.

Serves 6

1 roasting chicken (approximately 2 kg/ 4 lb 8 oz), skinned

100 g/3½ oz/7 tbsp butter

1 tsp salt

Orange, to garnish (optional)

For the stuffing

½ tsp good-quality saffron strands

1 orange

1 lemon

4 tbsp green raisins (or any other dried fruit)

200 g/7 oz semi-dried, pitted apricots, cut into small pieces

6 tbsp oil

3 dried red chillis, cut into small pieces

5 garlic cloves, finely chopped

1 small onion, finely chopped

In a bowl, infuse the saffron strands in 10 tbsp tepid water. Set aside. Using a vegetable peeler, peel the zest from the orange and lemon, then slice each piece into long, thin strips. Place the zest strips in a bowl and cover with hot water. Set aside. Place the raisins and apricots in a bowl and squeeze over the orange and lemon juice.

In a frying pan (skillet), heat the oil over a moderate heat. Add the dried red chillis, garlic and onion. Gently fry until the mixture starts to colour. Drain the raisins and apricots from the juice and add to the pan along with the citrus zest strips and 5 tbsp of the saffron water. Place over a low–moderate heat and reduce until most of the liquid has evaporated. Season the stuffing to taste. Remove from the heat and leave to cool.

Preheat the oven to 190°C/375°F/Gas Mark 5. Fill the cavity of the chicken with as much stuffing as possible, then tie it into shape. Place the chicken in a roasting tray and press any leftover stuffing around the bird. Brush the chicken with some of the remaining saffron water. Try to make sure some saffron strands stick to the surface of the chicken as this looks attractive once roasted. Melt the butter and brush it over the chicken, then season with salt.

As the chicken is skinless, wrap it in greased foil to prevent it from drying out. Place the foil-wrapped chicken in the preheated oven for 1½–2 hours. For the last 30 minutes of the cooking time, remove the foil. If you are roasting a chicken with the skin on, there is no need to use foil.

Remove the chicken from the oven. Pour the remaining saffron water over the chicken and leave it rest for 10 minutes before serving. To serve, garnish with oranges slices, if preferred.

Kofta Pulao
Meatball pulao

In South Asia there are some classic meat and rice combinations. Biryani is one, but it is a dish that takes time and practice to perfect. Kofta Pulao is another, and a good alternative when entertaining. Simple to prepare, Kofta Pulao requires no last-minute cooking or tweaking, but looks very grand and impressive despite the simplicity of cooking. For this recipe, I have used turkey mince – possibly an unusual choice, but turkey is not only for Thanksgiving or Christmas. I have used cranberries and pistachios to garnish the dish, so this could well be an alternative festive lunch dish. Of course, you could use any other minced or ground meat to make this dish and the koftas can be made the day before, refrigerated and heated before being added to the pulao.

Serves 10–12

For the kofta

1 slice of bread

1 kg/2 lb 4 oz/4½ cups minced (ground) turkey

1 tsp ground coriander

½ tsp ground cumin

1 tsp Kashmiri chilli powder (or paprika)

1 tbsp ground garam masala (see page 14)

1 tsp each of white pepper and salt

1 egg, beaten

Oil, for deep frying

For the pulao

600 g/1 lb 5 oz/3 cups basmati rice

6 tbsp ghee

2 medium onions, thinly sliced into rings

1 piece cassia bark, 5 cm/2 inches long

4 each of green cardamom pods and cloves

2 large Indian bay leaves

To garnish

Cranberries

Pistachio slivers

To make the kofta, in a shallow dish, put the slice of bread in water. Remove the bread from the dish and squeeze out the water. Break the soaked bread into small pieces in a bowl. Add all the other kofta ingredients, except the oil, and mix together. Take a handful of the kofta mixture and roll into small balls (2 cm/¾ inch in diameter). Following the instructions on page 77, test-fry one kofta, then adjust the seasoning before rolling and deep frying the remaining mixture.

Wash the basmati rice in several changes of cold running water until it runs clear. Place in a bowl with 2 tsp salt and soak in fresh water for 1 hour. Rinse the rice again and spread it out on paper towels to dry.

In a heavy-based, deep pan that has a tight-fitting lid, heat the ghee over a medium heat. Add the onions to the pan and fry gently, stirring occasionally, until golden brown and caramelized (see page 11). Using a slotted spoon, remove the onions from the oil and place on a plate to drain. Spread the onions across the plate so they crisp as they cool.

Put the kettle on to boil. Using the ghee left in the pan, add the cassia bark, cardamom pods, cloves and bay and cook, stirring, for 1 minute. Immediately add the rice to the pan. Stir for 1 minute to coat the rice in the spice-infused oil, then return the caramelized onions to the pan with 1 tbsp salt. Cover with 1.2 litres/40 fl oz/5 cups boiling water from the kettle. Bring the water back to the boil, then lower the heat, cover, and cook for 20 minutes. When the water has been absorbed by the rice, remove from the heat. Wrap the pan in a thick dish towel, then set aside.

To serve, warm the koftas in a low oven. Layer them with the rice so the pulao is studded with koftas. Garnish with cranberries and pistachios.

Tamatar Gosht
Lamb in tomato gravy

This is a classic lamb dish cooked in many South Asian households. There are endless variations on this recipe; you should feel free to make this your 'own' signature dish by tweaking proportions and adding potatoes, whole shallots or even a swirl of clotted cream before serving. As with many meat recipes in this book, you can swap the lamb for beef or chicken. If you decide to cook chicken, adding ½ tsp dried fenugreek leaves (kasuri methi) imparts a wonderful flavour to this dish.

Serves 6

6 garlic cloves

1 piece of fresh ginger, 5 cm/2 inches long

2 dried red chillis

4 tbsp vegetable oil

300 g/10½ oz onions, thinly sliced into half moons

1 tsp ground turmeric

3 tsp ground coriander

1 tsp ground cumin

2 tsp salt

1 kg/2 lb 4 oz diced lamb

3 x 400-g/14-oz tins chopped tomatoes or 900 g/2 lb fresh tomatoes, chopped

½ tsp sugar (optional)

To garnish

Green chillis

Chopped coriander (cilantro) leaves

Grind the garlic, ginger and dried red chillis with a splash of water to make a smooth paste.

In a pan that has a lid, heat the oil over a medium–high heat. Add the onions. Cook, stirring, until they become golden brown. Add the garlic, ginger and chilli paste and stir for 3 minutes. Next, add the ground turmeric (and kasuri methi, if cooking chicken), followed by the ground coriander, ground cumin and salt.

Add the diced lamb (or other meat) to the pan and seal with the onion and spice mix. Add the chopped tomatoes, stir for few minutes, then add enough water to cover the meat. Bring the water to the boil, cover with a lid and simmer until the meat is cooked. This may take anything from 30 minutes for chicken pieces to 1 hour for diced lamb.

The gravy should be glossy and thick. If there is any excess water in the pan, remove the lid and allow the water to evaporate.

Before serving, taste to check the seasoning and adjust as necessary. I add a touch of sugar as I like a slightly sweet and tangy flavour to the gravy.

To serve, garnish with whole green chillis and chopped coriander leaves.

Raan
Whole leg of lamb

Occasionally you need to make a showstopper dish. Raan is usually made in family dawaats, or feasts. Do not be daunted by the list of ingredients; this is a surprisingly easy dish to make as the leg of lamb can be roasted whole in the oven. In my family, the Raan is usually cooked over a wood fire in a giant pot that fits three or four lamb legs. In Calcutta we usually use legs of the local khasi (mutton), which are quite small and so, for a large family gathering, several legs need to be cooked. I have simplified this recipe by using one larger leg of lamb. I enjoy this lamb with a simple Kachumber salad (page 166) and Lachedar Parathas (pages 167–9).

Serves 6

200 g/7 oz ghee, melted

100 g/3½ oz onions, thinly sliced into half moons

100 g/3½ oz/scant ½ cup full-fat natural (plain) yogurt

3 tsp salt

2 tsp chilli powder

2 tbsp ground coriander

1 tsp ground garam masala (see page 14)

1 tsp ground white pepper

4 tbsp gram (chickpea or besan) flour

1 tbsp ground almonds

1 tbsp ground poppy seeds

¼ tsp ground cardamom

¼ tsp ground mace

4 tbsp grated raw green papaya

10 strands good-quality saffron, infused in 1 tbsp tepid milk

6 tbsp clotted (heavy) cream (or reduced milk khoa)

3 tbsp kewra water (pandan or screw pine essence)

1.5 kg/3 lb 5 oz leg of lamb

In a deep saucepan, heat the ghee over a medium–high heat. Add the onions to the pan and gently fry until golden brown and caramelized (see page 11). Using a slotted spoon, remove the onions from the pan and place on a plate to drain. Set the ghee aside to use later.

Grind the browned onions to a paste. Place the yogurt in a large bowl and mix in the ground onions with all the other ingredients except the lamb leg. Stir until the ingredients are evenly combined.

Place the leg of lamb in a tray. Using the tip of a sharp knife, make small slits all over the leg of lamb and then rub in the yogurt marinade. Leave to marinate for 3 hours in the refrigerator. Take it out and repeat the process – make more slits all over the lamb leg and reapply the marinade to the meat, reusing any marinade that has collected in the tray. Leave to marinate for a further 3 hours in the refrigerator. Alternatively, marinate the lamb overnight in the refrigerator.

Take the lamb out of the refrigerator 1 hour before cooking to allow it to come to room temperature. Preheat the oven to 200°C/400°F/Gas Mark 6.

Place the lamb in the preheated oven and cook for 20 minutes, then lower the temperature to 180°C/350°F/Gas Mark 4 and cook for 1 hour 40 minutes, basting regularly with the ghee used to fry the onions. To check whether the lamb is done to your liking, using clean hands, touch the top of the thickest part of the lamb leg. If it feels soft to the touch, the lamb is rare. If it feels springy, it is medium. If it feels firm, it is well done.

To serve, place the whole leg of lamb on a serving plate and carve into thick slices at the table.

Hyderabadi Dalcha
Tangy meat with lentils

The quantity of meat needed for this recipe is very small, making it perfect for entertaining on a budget. Plus, it can be made using a cheap cut, such as a shank, neck or shoulder. Meat that takes longer to cook – which often means it is cheaper – has a lot more flavour than expensive joints of meat.

Serves 6

225 g/8 oz/1⅓ cups masoor dal (red lentils)

½ tsp ground turmeric

4 tsp salt

4 tbsp ghee or vegetable oil

1 Indian bay leaf

1 piece cassia bark, 2.5 cm/1 inch long (see page 13)

6 green cardamom pods

1 medium onion, thinly sliced into half moons

225 g/8 oz lamb shoulder, neck chops or shanks, cut into small chunks

1 tbsp crushed garlic

1 tbsp ground ginger

1 tsp chilli powder

2 tbsp tomato purée (tomato paste)

1 tbsp tamarind pulp (or 2 tbsp lemon juice)

For the tempering

60 ml/2 fl oz/4 tbsp melted ghee or vegetable oil

2 garlic cloves, cut into slivers

½ tsp cumin seeds

2 dried red chillis

8–10 fresh curry leaves

Wash the lentils in cold running water, then place in a bowl and soak for 20 minutes in more fresh cold water.

Drain the lentils and place in a heavy-based pan that has a lid. Add the ground turmeric and 1 tsp of the salt. Pour in enough water to cover the lentils by 7.5 cm/3 inches. Place over a medium heat and bring to a simmer. Cover with a lid and simmer gently for 30 minutes or until the lentils are tender. Leave the lentils to cool a little and then grind to a purée using a whisk or food processor.

While the lentils are cooking, prepare the meat. In a wide-based pan, heat the ghee or oil over a medium–high heat. Add the bay leaf, cassia bark and cardamom pods. Stir for a few seconds, then add the onion and fry gently until caramelized (see page 11).

Now, add the meat and seal on all sides. Next, add the garlic, ginger, chilli powder and remaining 3 tsp of the salt. Stir for 1 minute to allow the spices to brown. Now pour in 250 ml/8½ fl oz/1 cup cold water, bring to a simmer and cook very gently for 1–1¼ hours, or until the meat is tender.

Remove the lid and allow any excess liquid to evaporate and the oil to seep to the edges of the pan. Add the lentil purée to the meat, stir to mix and taste for seasoning. Add the tomato purée and the tamarind pulp (or lemon juice) and stir.

In a small frying pan (skillet), heat the ghee or oil over a high heat. Working quickly so the tempering does not burn, add the garlic, cumin seeds, dried red chillis and curry leaves. Cook for 1 minute, then pour the tempering oil, garlic and spices over the warm dal in the pan. Next, take a spoonful of the dal and place it in the frying pan to absorb any remaining oil – take care whilst doing this as the oil may splutter – then tip the spoonful of dal from the frying pan back into the main dal pan. Taste to check the seasoning and adjust as necessary.

Kache Keeme Ka Kabab
Tray-baked beef kabab

This kabab can be made in advance of your guests arriving and left covered to stay warm in a very low oven or reheated when your guests arrive. The advantage of this kabab is that it does not require you to make individual portions or spend time skewering meat. The kabab can simply be cut into squares and served.

Serves 8

Vegetable oil, for greasing

1 kg/2 lb 4 oz lean finely minced (ground) beef

1 large onion, finely chopped

1 tbsp fresh ginger paste

½ tbsp garlic paste

4 green chillis, finely chopped

1 tsp crushed black peppercorns

2 tsp salt

4 tbsp melted unsalted butter

To garnish

A handful of fresh coriander (cilantro) leaves

Lemon slices

Grease a 25 x 38-cm/10 x 15-inch baking tray with vegetable oil. (The tray needs to hold 1 kg/2 lb 4 oz of minced (ground) beef spread in a 1-cm/½-inch layer and fit under the grill (broiler), so check the capacity of your tray and whether it fits first.)

Place all the kabab ingredients, except the melted butter, in a large bowl and mix together thoroughly. Pack the kabab mixture tightly in the greased tray, spreading it evenly and making sure the meat is 1 cm/½ inch thick. (It is important to keep the meat the same 1-cm/½-inch thickness across the tray – if the layer of meat is too thin it will burn, and if it too thick it will be undercooked.) Brush the top of the meat evenly with the melted butter.

Preheat the grill (broiler) to a moderate heat. Grill (broil) the kabab in the baking tray for 20–30 minutes or until the top is crusty and the meat cooked through. (Make sure the tray is not too close to the heat source otherwise the top surface of the kabab may burn – 10 cm/4 inches away from the heat is ideal.)

Once cooked, leave to cool slightly and then, using a wet, sharp knife, cut the grilled kabab meat into 8 equal pieces in the tray.

Serve immediately while hot, garnished with fresh coriander leaves and lemon slices.

Bihari Kabab
Barbecued beef strips

This is one of my favourite kababs, which my mother serves at every family gathering. We have an open courtyard at home in India and invariably everyone ends up standing around the barbecue, watching the kabab cook. The ideal way to cook this kabab is over coals, although it also works with a grill or broiler. The mustard oil is important in this dish and worth seeking out in Asian grocery stores, although olive oil is a good alternative. Raw green papaya can be found in both Indian and Thai food stores.

Serves 6–8

2 kg/4 lb 8 oz lean beef, such as sirloin

8 tbsp grated raw green papaya

6 tbsp garlic paste

12 tbsp fresh ginger paste

3 tbsp salt

4 tbsp vegetable oil

500 g/1 lb 2 oz onions, thinly sliced into half moons

12 tbsp poppy seeds

6 tbsp whole black peppercorns

2 tbsp chilli powder

250 ml/8½ fl oz/1 cup mustard oil (or olive oil)

250 ml/8½ fl oz/1 cup natural (plain) yogurt (not low-fat)

Cut the beef into 3-mm (¹/₈-inch) thick slices, then each slice into 10-cm (8-inch) strips. (The beef will be easier to slice if first placed in the freezer for about 30 minutes.)

Place the beef strips in a non-reactive container with a lid and cover with the grated papaya, garlic and ginger pastes and salt. Cover the container and leave to marinate for 2 hours.

In a frying pan (skillet), heat the vegetable oil over a medium–high heat. Add the sliced onions to the pan and fry gently, stirring occasionally, until light brown. Using a slotted spoon, remove the onions from the oil, leaving as much of the oil in the pan as possible to baste the kabab, and place on paper towels to drain. Grind the onions to a paste.

In a dry frying pan (skillet), toast the poppy seeds until they darken. Using a pestle and mortar, grind the poppy seeds to a powder with the peppercorns. In a small bowl, combine this powder with the onion paste, chilli powder and mustard oil and yogurt. Pour this spiced yogurt over the beef strips in the container and place in the refrigerator to marinate for a further 6 hours or overnight, if possible.

When ready to cook the kababs, remove the beef from the refrigerator to bring to room temperature. Thread the beef onto long, thin metal skewers, skewering down the centre of the strips to ensure even cooking. Pack the beef strips tightly onto the skewers. Cook the kababs on a barbecue over hot coals or under a medium–high grill (broiler), turning frequently and basting with the onion-infused oil.

Serve with lime wedges to squeeze over and a crisp Kachumber salad.

Not all Indian cooking is the same

The food of India is an amalgamation of various regional cooking
traditions and ingredients. To understand the food of any Indian
region, you first need to understand the history of that area. In
this book, I have included a range of dishes that are regional
speciality dishes, such as Chicken Chaap (page 136), Tamatar Ka
Cutt (page 80), Rogni Roti (page 53) and Yakhni Pulao (page 138).

Sometimes the name given to a dish is an indication of its roots,
like Sheermal (page 117) and Kofta (page 77). Other times it
is ingredients like the panchporan five-seed spice mix used in
the Tamatar Chutney (page 160) that indicates the dish is from
the east of India, where this spice is used heavily. The Mughal
influence is predominantly a Persian culinary tradition; their
food is lighter, more fragrant and often missing ground turmeric
and cumin in the spicing.

Dals are also an indication of regional variations. Kali Dal (page 158) is a heavier and richer dal more suited to the north of India, where winter can be icily cold and the protein-packed, warming dal is appreciated. The Masoor Dal (page 39), which is more commonly used in central and eastern India, is much lighter and easier to digest and so better suited to people leaving in hot, humid regions. There is no generic Indian food: if you travel 30 minutes in any direction you will find differences in the way dishes are prepared. Even how a dal is tempered.

Lastly, because of religious differences, there are variations in the dishes eaten in families. Across India, some religions avoid certain foods. But the conception that the majority of Indians are vegetarian is a myth.

Narangi Korma
Orange korma

My paternal great-grandfather, Lieutenant Colonel Sir Muhammad Ahmed Said Khan, Nawab of Chhatari, played an active role in the transition of India from colonial rule to independence. Under British India, he was the only Indian to hold the post of Governor of United Provinces of Agra and Oudh, later becoming the first Chief Minister of United Provinces and then Prime Minister to the last Nizam of Hyderabad from 1941–46 and again in 1947.

Organizing banquets for visiting dignitaries and royalty was an important part of his life. India in the 1930s and 40s went through enormous political change; the dark shadow of partition loomed on the horizon. Many discussions took place in our home between Indian and British political parties. My great-grandfather travelled to England in 1930 and 1931 to attend the Round Table Conferences on Indian constitutional reform, organized by the British government. He travelled by ship and then overland through Europe. On his return, a new ingredient was added to a dish, specially prepared for royal banquets. Oranges joined cashew nuts in this yogurt-based chicken korma and then were grown in our fruit orchards, surrounding the fortress of Chhatari. This recipe was given to me by Muhammad Babu, son of the head cook of our family kitchen during my great-grandfather's lifetime. I remember clearly eating this orange korma at a banquet to celebrate my great-grandfather's ninetieth birthday.

Serves 6

3 large oranges

8 tbsp melted ghee

150 g/5½ oz lotus seeds (makhana)

200 g/7 oz onions, thinly sliced

1 tbsp garlic paste

1 tbsp fresh ginger paste

1 tsp salt

2 tbsp ground coriander

1 tsp chilli powder

50 g/2 oz/¹/₃ cup cashew nuts

50 g/2 oz/¹/₃ cup almonds

180 g/6 ½ oz/¾ cup natural (plain) yogurt

250 ml/8½ fl oz/1 cup water

1 tsp ground garam masala (see page 14)

½ tsp ground turmeric

1 kg/2 lb 4 oz skinless, bone-in chicken thighs

1 large Indian bay leaf

¼ tsp sugar

Wash the oranges thoroughly. Cut one orange in half, from top to bottom, then cut one half into segments with the peel still on. Cover and set aside. Peel the remaining oranges and cut the rind into thin slivers. Squeeze the juice from the oranges and set aside.

In a small pan, heat 1 tbsp of the ghee and fry the lotus seeds. Set aside a small handful of the fried lotus seeds for the garnish. Mix the remaining lotus seeds with a splash of water and grind to a paste.

In a pan, heat the remaining ghee and fry the onions until they are brown and caramelized (see page 11). Remove with a slotted spoon to a plate to drain. Using a food processor, blitz the onions to a paste. Set aside the remaining ghee in the pan to use later to cook the chicken.

Using a food processor, blitz the nuts to a powder. Add the ground nuts to the yogurt and then thin the mixture down with a little water.

While the onions are frying, mix the lotus seed paste, garlic and ginger pastes, salt, ground coriander, chilli powder, almond and cashew nut powdered with the yogurt and the water. Add the browned onion paste to the yogurt mixture.

Cut the chicken thighs in half. Put the pan in which the onions were cooked back on a medium heat. Add the bay leaf, garam masala and turmeric followed by the chicken pieces and seal both sides. Immediately pour the yogurt mixture over the chicken and let the contents come to a boil. Cover, lower the heat and let it cook on a simmer. After 20 minutes, add the strips of orange rind to the chicken. Add the sugar and half the orange slices to the chicken at the very end.

Taste to check the seasoning and adjust as necessary.

When ready to serve, garnish with the remaining orange segments and the reserved fried lotus seeds.

Dum Ki Machli
Whole baked fish in spiced yogurt

In Calcutta we have a wonderful fish known as bhekti – Asian sea bass or barramundi – which my family cooks whole. The fish is marinated in spiced yogurt for several hours, then wrapped in foil and baked. This dish can be made using any decent-sized fish, such as sea bass or trout. Ideally, find a single fish weighing 1.5 kg/3 lb 5 oz, however you can use two smaller fish if more convenient.

Serves 6

4 tbsp melted butter

4 medium onions, finely chopped

4 garlic cloves, finely sliced

1½ tsp ground turmeric

2 tsp salt

1½ tsp freshly ground black pepper

1 tsp sugar

100 g/3½ oz fresh coriander (cilantro) leaves, finely chopped

3 green chillis

750 g/1 lb 10 oz/2½ cups natural (plain) yogurt

1 whole fish, such as sea bass or trout, (approximately 1.5 kg/3 lb 5 oz, gutted, scaled and ready to cook)

To garnish

Lemon slices

A few sprigs of fresh coriander (cilantro) leaves

2 tbsp chopped grapes (optional)

In a pan, heat the butter over a medium–high heat. Add the onions and garlic. Cook, stirring, until they just start to colour – this should take about 4 minutes – do not let the butter burn. Lower the heat to medium, add the ground turmeric, salt, ground pepper and sugar and cook for a further 4 minutes. Take the pan off the heat and leave to cool. Transfer the onion mixture to a food processor, add the chopped coriander and chillis, then blend to a paste. Stir the paste into the yogurt and pour over the fish. Leave to marinate for at least 4 hours.

When ready to bake the fish, preheat the oven to 180°C/350°F/Gas Mark 4. Place a sheet of parchment paper on top of a sheet of foil. Wrap the fish in the paper and foil, then place in a roasting tray. Bake in the preheated oven for 45–60 minutes, depending on the type and size of fish.

When the fish is cooked, garnish with the chopped grapes, lemon slices and coriander leaves.

Macher Jhol
Bengali fish curry

In Bengal, the fish used for this recipe would be Rohu, a local carp, which requires some skill to debone. In a large family gathering, it makes sense to use fish that has been filleted to make things easier for both you and your guests. If you can source a good mustard oil, it gives this dish a wonderful flavour.

Serves 6 as a main course or 12 as part of a multi-course meal

1.5 kg/3 lb 5 oz skinless, boneless fish fillets, such as cod or halibut

3 tsp salt

1½ tsp ground turmeric

6 tbsp vegetable oil or mustard oil

1 large white onion, finely grated

4 garlic cloves, crushed

1 piece ginger, 2.5 cm/1 inch long, crushed to a paste

1 tbsp ground coriander

1 tsp ground cumin

1 tsp chilli powder

3 tbsp tomato purée (tomato paste)

200 g/7 oz tomatoes, cut into 2.5-cm/1-inch cubes

600 ml/1 pint/2½ cup warm water

½ tsp sugar

To garnish

Green chillis

A few sprigs of fresh coriander (cilantro) leaves

Cut the fish fillets into 12 equal portions. Mix 1 tsp of the salt and 1 tsp of the ground turmeric, then rub on all sides of the fish and set aside for 30 minutes.

In a shallow saucepan, heat 5 tbsp of the oil over a medium–high heat. If you are using mustard oil, heat the oil until it is smoking hot – this removes the bitter pungency of the oil – then bring it down to a medium–high heat. Add the fish to the pan and fry to seal each piece, but do not let the fillets cook through. Remove from the pan to a plate and set aside.

Add the onion, garlic and ginger to the pan and cook, stirring, for 2 minutes over a medium–high heat. If the paste is burning or sticking to the base of the pan, add a splash of water. Add the remaining salt and ground turmeric, followed by the ground coriander, ground cumin, chilli powder, tomato purée and diced tomatoes. Pour in 600 ml/1 pint/2½ cups warm water and cook for 5 minutes. Keeping the pan on a medium–high heat, let the liquid reduce for 15 minutes or until the oil comes to the surface and seeps to the sides of the pan.

Gently return the fish fillets to the pan and cover with the gravy, ensuring all sides of each fillet are cooking evenly. If possible, cook the fish fillets in a single layer in the pan as this will prevent them from breaking up into flakes. Lower the heat, add the sugar and cook, covered, until the fillets are cook through – this should take no longer than 5 minutes.

To serve, garnish the fish with whole green chillis and sprigs of fresh coriander leaves.

Kali Dal
Black lentils V

This is a dal from North India, where it is more commonly known as 'Maa Ki Dal'. The lentil used here is called whole urad dal. It is more common to eat this dal with roti – Punjab is the 'bread basket' of India, where most farmers in the state grow wheat – but you could eat this dal with rice, too. The lentils, along with the kidney beans, must be soaked overnight. Please do not be tempted to use tinned beans as they do not have the same texture or taste as rehydrated, and slow-cooked dried beans. This is not a quick recipe: the longer the dal cooks for, the better the flavour and texture. However, the good news is that you can put the dal on to cook and then leave it, giving it only the occasional stir.

Serves 8

600 g/1 lb 5 oz/3 cups whole urad dal (black lentils)

150 g/5½ oz/1 cup dried red kidney beans

2 tbsp crushed garlic

2 tbsp grated fresh ginger

500 g/1 lb 2 oz tomatoes, chopped

200 g/7 oz/1¾ sticks butter, cut into pieces, plus an extra knob to finish

A pinch each of sugar and salt (adjust to taste)

4 tbsp double (heavy) cream

For the tempering

2 tbsp vegetable oil

1 medium red onion, thinly sliced

1 tbsp cumin seeds

2 tsp chilli powder

To garnish

Fresh ginger slivers

A handful of coriander (cilantro) leaves, chopped

Wash the lentils in cold running water, then place in a large pan with 4 litres/7 pints/1 gallon plus 1 cup cold water and soak overnight.

Place the dried kidney beans in a separate pan with cold water, covering the beans by 10 cm/4 inches, and soak overnight.

When ready to cook, rinse the lentils and kidney beans in fresh water, drain, then place in a heavy-based pan with more water, covering the lentils and beans by 5 cm/2 inches. Do not add too much water initially as this will thin the dal. Bring to the boil, then lower the heat and simmer for 2 hours. During the cooking, if the dal appears to be drying out or sticking to the base of the pan, add 2–3 tbsp hot water.

After 2 hours, add the garlic, ginger, tomatoes and butter to the dal and cook for a further 30 minutes. Once the dal is cooked, place it in a bowl and keep warm while preparing the tempering.

In a small frying pan (skillet), heat the vegetable oil over a high heat. Working quickly so the tempering does not burn, add the red onion, cumin seeds and, finally, the chilli powder. Cook for 1 minute, then pour the tempering oil, onion and spices over the warm dal in the pan. Next, take a spoonful of the dal and place it in the frying pan to absorb any remaining oil – take care whilst doing this as the oil may splutter – then tip the spoonful of dal from the frying pan back into the main dal pan. Season with a pinch of sugar and salt, taste to check the seasoning and adjust as necessary.

To serve, drizzle the dal with the double cream and add a knob of butter. Finally, garnish with ginger slivers and chopped coriander leaves.

Rajma
Spiced kidney beans in gravy <u>v</u>

Rajma Chawal is a family favourite in India. Rajma is usually served with rice, or 'Chawal'. It is in the same league as 'Dal Bhaat', which is dal and rice. Both are classic Indian comfort foods. The only Western equivalent that springs to mind is hot buttered toast. Remember, you do need to start the preparation for this dish the night before, washing and soaking the beans in plenty of cold water overnight.

Serves 8

1 kg/2 lb 4 oz/5 cups dried red kidney beans

1 tsp ground turmeric

1 tsp chilli powder

150 ml/5 fl oz/²/₃ cup melted ghee

1 large onion, finely chopped

1 piece ginger, 5 cm/2 inches long, peeled and grated

2 green chillis, thickly sliced

1 x 400-g/14-oz tin chopped tomatoes

3 tsp salt

500 ml/17 fl oz/2 cups warm water

1 tbsp ground garam masala (see page 14)

Place the dried red kidney beans in a pan with cold water, covering the beans by 10 cm/4 inches, and soak overnight.

When ready to cook, rinse the soaked kidney beans in fresh cold water, drain, then place in a heavy-based pan that has a lid with another 3 litres/5¼ pints/3 quarts and ¾ cup fresh cold water. Add the ground turmeric and chilli powder, then bring to the boil over a high heat. Once the kidney beans are boiling, maintain at a boil for 5–10 minutes. Regularly skim off any foam that floats to the surface of the water. Once the boiling water is clear of foam, lower the heat, cover with a lid and simmer for at least 1 hour.

Once the kidney beans are cooked, remove the lid and increase the heat to high until any remaining liquid has evaporated. Using the back of a wooden spoon, break up some of the beans for a thicker texture.

In a frying pan (skillet), heat the ghee and add the onion, ginger, green chillis, tomatoes and salt. Cook until the ghee separates from the onion mixture. Pour this onion mixture into the pan with the kidney beans and stir to mix well. Add 500 ml/17 fl oz/2 cups warm water and continue to stir. The bean mixture should be thick but moist. If you feel the texture is too dry, add a splash more water. Continue to stir until the beans appear to have a glaze, which is a sign they are ready.

Before serving, taste to check the seasoning and adjust as necessary. Finally, add the ground garam masala and gently stir to combine.

Tamatar Ki Chutney
Tomato chutney with prunes and apricots v

The spice infusion used in this chutney is panchporan, a five-seed spice used extensively in eastern India, especially Bengal. The combination of fennel, fenugreek, cumin, nigella and mustard seeds gives this dish a unique spice flavour which combined with dried red chillis, and sugar, results in a tangy, sweet and spicy chutney that goes with everything – even cheese on toast. Tamatar chutney is usually the final savoury course at a Bengali wedding, a palate cleanser of sorts, before the all-important arrival of desserts to the table. In Bengal you often find dried mangoes or mango leather in a chutney. The texture of the dried apricots in this recipe is similar to those mangoes. The Durga Puja (see page 73) tamatar chutney which was served free to the entire neighbourhood with rice and a vegetable side was often much simpler (a cost consideration) and would only contain raisins.

Serves 6–8

2 tbsp vegetable oil

4 dried red chillis

½ tsp panchporan (see page 15)

6 garlic cloves, crushed

1 piece fresh ginger, 2.5 cm/1 inch long, peeled and cut into thin slivers

2 x 400-g/14-oz tins chopped tomatoes

2 tbsp sugar

1 tsp salt

4 dried prunes, quartered

6 dried apricots, quartered

2 green chillis, to garnish

Warm the oil in a shallow pan over a medium–high heat. Add the dried red chillis, followed by the panchporan. When the mustard seeds in the panchporan mix start to pop, add the garlic and ginger. Fry gently for 1 minute, but do not allow the garlic and ginger to colour.

Add the chopped tomatoes, followed by the sugar and salt. Bring the tomatoes to a boil, then lower the heat to medium; the mixture should no longer be spitting but the tomatoes should still be boiling.

After 10 minutes, add the prunes and apricots. Continue to cook the chutney until there is a glaze on the surface and the tomato juice has reduced, about 15–20 minutes.

Taste the chutney and adjust the seasoning with salt or sugar, if necessary.

To serve, garnish with whole green chillis.

This chutney keeps for a week in the refrigerator.

Navratan Pulao
Pulao rice with nine jewels V

Navratan means 'nine jewels' and describes the traditional way that gemstones are set together in gold to make a colourful cluster. A navratan set is considered auspicious by many families and, in certain regions of India, it is always one of the jewellery sets gifted by the family on the marriage to a new bride. To mimic the gem-clustered jewellery, this dish contains nine coloured ingredients set against the grains of white rice. This is an intensely fragrant and visually stunning rice dish, and the nuts, berries, carrots, orange zest and juice give this rice a fruity sweetness. The best way to serve this is with roast beef, such as Dum Gosht (see page 94) or Dum Ki Machli (see page 154) with the Tomato Raita (see page 111).

Serves 6–8

600 g/1 lb 5 oz/3 cups basmati rice

4 tbsp salt

1 tsp good-quality saffron strands

70 g/2½ oz/½ cup whole almonds

70 g/2½ oz/½ cup whole shelled pistachios

35 g/1¼ oz/¼ cup green raisins

35 g/1¼ oz/¼ cup golden sultanas

90 g/3 oz/¾ cup unsweetened dried cranberries

2 large oranges

9 tbsp ghee or melted butter

3 large carrots, peeled and cut into even-sized matchsticks

4 tbsp granulated sugar

35 g/1¼ oz/¼ cup cashew nuts

2 medium Indian bay leaves

1 piece cassia bark, 7.5 cm/3 inches long (see page 13)

6 green cardamom pods

2 tbsp kewra water (pandan or screw pine essence) (optional)

1 tsp fresh or dried rose petals, to garnish

Wash the rice in several changes of cold running water until it runs clear, then place in a bowl with 1 tbsp of the salt and soak for 30 minutes in fresh cold water.

In a bowl, infuse the saffron strands in 4 tbsp tepid water. Set aside

In separate bowls, soak the almonds, pistachios, raisins, sultanas and cranberries in cold water for 1 hour. Drain, skin the nuts, then cut into slivers. (If short on time, buy pre-cut almond and pistachio slivers.)

Using a vegetable peeler or sharp knife, peel the zest from the oranges. Wash the zest well and then, in a pan of water, boil the zest to remove any bitter aftertaste. Repeat this two or three times in fresh water. Drain, then leave to cool.

Next, in a small non-stick pan, heat 3 tbsp of the ghee or melted butter. Fry the carrot matchsticks in the pan, adding splashes of cold water to prevent them from sticking. It is important not to over-stir or overcook the carrots. As they cook, sprinkle 1½ tbsp of the sugar over the carrots, reduce the heat, then when they look caramelized, test to check they are cooked. Remove the carrots to a plate. Spread them out so they do not continue to cook or soften.

Drain the raisins, sultanas and cranberries. Dry them on paper towels so they don't splutter in the oil when fried. In the same pan used to cook the carrots, heat another 2 tbsp ghee or butter over a medium heat. First, add the cranberries, stirring quickly to prevent them burning. Remove to a plate.

Add the almonds, again stirring, then remove to a plate when they change colour and look almost translucent. Next, add the pistachios. Again, flash fry the pistachios, then remove them to the plate. Lower the heat, then add the cashew nuts. Flash fry the cashew nuts, again removing to the plate when done. Finally, add the raisins and sultanas, flash fry and then remove to the plate to drain.

The 'jewels' are now ready. If any ingredient has burnt during the flash frying – and you do not have any more in your kitchen – leave that 'jewel' out. None of your guests are going to count how many ingredients are in the pulao, but they may notice a burnt raisin.

In a large pan, bring 2 litres/68 fl oz/8½ cups water to a boil. Drain the rice and add to the pan with the remaining 3 tbsp salt. Cook for 30 minutes until the rice is only three-quarters cooked and still with some bite to it, similar to al dente pasta. Drain and rinse the rice under running cold water in a fine sieve or muslin-lined colander to stop the rice cooking. Spread the rice out over a tray and leave to cool.

In a large pan with a tight-fitting lid, heat the remaining 4 tbsp ghee or butter. (If planning to finish the dish in the oven, use an ovenproof pan.) Add the bay leaf, cassia bark and cardamom pods. Add the rice and stir to coat the grains in the spice-infused ghee. Dissolve the remaining 2½ tbsp sugar in 75 ml/2½ fl oz/⅓ cup warm water. Make a few holes in the rice and pour in the saffron water and sugar water. If using the kewra water, add this now.

If cooking on the hob (stove), tightly seal the pan with the lid and place over a medium heat. After 10 minutes, lift the lid and layer the carrots, orange zest, nuts, cranberries and raisins on top, reserving a handful of each 'jewel' to garnish. Replace the lid. Reduce the heat to low and leave for 30–35 minutes.

If cooking in the oven, preheat the oven to 200°C/400°F/Gas Mark 6. Place the pan in the oven. After 10 minutes, add the 'jewels' (remembering to reserve some for a garnish). Reduce the heat to 150°C/300°F/Gas Mark 2 and cook for a further 30–35 minutes.

To serve, garnish with rose petals and 'jewels'.

Alvida Haji Saheb

This year, my family cook, Haji Saheb, who had been unwell for the past few years, passed away. He was the person who taught me how to cook many of the recipes in this book. I wish him 'Alvida' or 'Farewell'. I imagine Haji Saheb in heaven, wearing his loose-flowing kurta and white pajamas, organizing dawaats for thousands of people with his customary calmness and polite mannerisms. Feeding people was his passion. Those in heaven now have one of the best cooks in their midst.

I spent most of my childhood playing cricket with my brother and neighbours in the gardens, right outside the kitchen where Haji Saheb cooked. I was never tempted to venture inside to see what he was cooking. While I loved eating, I simply wasn't interested in learning how the food was made. My first real experience of watching a feast being prepared was when my sister got married. As the special guests sat down to eat at the wedding banquet, I was dispatched by my mother to the kitchen to help get platters of biryani out quickly. Dressed in traditional flowing silk and finery, I entered the kitchen looking for Haji Saheb. There I found him about to unseal a huge 'degh', or traditional pot, of biryani.

I had never witnessed a degh being opened before. As I watched Haji Saheb cut the seal and prise off the lid, I was mesmerized by the plumes of steam that rose from the degh and the fragrant aroma that enveloped the kitchen. While Haji Saheb spooned out the biryani onto ceremonial silver platters, he placed a few grains of rice in my hands. He had seen something in my eyes, he told me, which made him sure that one day I would make biryani even better than him. Those grains of rice, he believed, contained my destiny, which was to bring honour to my family by cooking rice that people would never forget.

Thank you, Haji Saheb, for patiently and lovingly teaching me all the family recipes when I returned to Calcutta in the summer of 1992. I wish you had seen Darjeeling Express and this cookbook. I have now written down your recipes, so I no longer need to memorize them and I can also share them with others.

Kachumber
Lemon and chilli-infused salad V

This is the perfect salad with Indian food: fresh and crunchy, it goes with anything. As long as you do not add the citrus dressing until the last moment, you can prepare this salad in advance and keep it in the refrigerator. If you want to omit any item from the ingredients list, simply add a little more of another ingredient to make up the deficit. It is important that all the main components going into the salad are cut the same size. This is always the first thing my mother notices; she thoroughly disapproves of an unevenly cut kachumber salad.

Serves 6–8

225 g/8 oz cucumber, cut into 5-mm/¼-inch cubes

225 g/8 oz tomatoes, cut to the same size as the cucumber

100 g/3½ oz red onions, cut to the same size as the cucumber

50 g/1¾ oz pomegranate seeds

2–3 green chillis, chopped

¼ tsp salt

4 tbsp lime or lemon juice

A few fresh mint sprigs, to garnish

In a salad bowl, combine the cucumber, tomatoes, onions, pomegranate seeds and chillis.

Season with salt, then dress the salad with lime or lemon juice.

Serve immediately, garnished with the fresh mint sprigs.

Lachedar Parathas
Layered ghee flatbreads V

Lachedar Parathas are special layered parathas served at grand family feasts, common at all the traditional Mughlai roadside restaurants in Calcutta. There are two ways of shaping these parathas; it is worth trying both methods to see which one works best for you. This paratha is made with enriched dough, usually using ghee. If you are vegan, replace the ghee with oil.

Serves 8

300 g/10½ oz/2¼ cups white unbleached flour

½ tsp baking powder

½ tsp salt

½ tsp sugar

3 tbsp melted ghee, unsalted butter or oil

For layering and frying

4 tbsp melted unsalted butter

Flour, for dusting

300 ml/10 fl oz/1¼ cups ghee or oil

Sift the flour, baking powder, salt and sugar into a large bowl. Add the 3 tbsp melted ghee, butter or oil and rub into the flour until it resembles breadcrumbs.

Gradually add 175 ml/6 fl oz/¾ cup warm water in dribbles until the dough is pliable but quite stiff. Depending on the flour used, you may not need all the water.

Turn the dough out onto a lightly floured work surface and knead for 10 minutes until it feels smooth and silky. Place in a lightly floured bowl, cover and leave to rest for 1–3 hours.

Once rested, divide the dough into eight equal-sized pieces. Take each piece and shape into a patty. Dust the patties lightly with flour and roll out to 18-cm/7-inch discs. Spread 1½ tsp of the extra melted unsalted butter over the top of each disc and dust lightly with some extra flour.

There are two ways to layer the paratha. For the first way (shown opposite), using a sharp knife, make a cut from the middle of the disc to the outer edge, then roll the paratha tightly from the cut to make a cone. Place the wide end or base on the work surface and press down to form a patty, this time with layers. For the second way, make small pleats in the disc like a paper fan, folding until you have one long pleated piece of dough. Curl the pleated dough into a circle to make a patty.

Once all the discs have been made into layered patties, cover and leave to rest for 2 hours.

Take the patties out of the refrigerator 10 minutes before you are ready to roll them, to bring them to room temperature. Dust the patties with flour and roll into 15-cm/6-inch discs. As you roll out each paratha, place them on a plate, laying parchment paper between each one to stop them sticking to each other.

In a shallow saucepan, heat 1 cm/½ inch of ghee or oil to 180°C/350°F. Carefully slide the paratha into the hot oil. Use the back of a slotted spoon to push the paratha down and keep it submerged in the hot oil. Fry on each side for 2 minutes until the surface is crisp and brown.

These parathas are best eaten when freshly fried. Often that is hard to do when entertaining and you have a lot of dishes to cook on the day of your party, so you can prepare these parathas in advance. Either make the patties the day before and refrigerate for up to 24 hours and then fry them on the day of the event or make and fry the parathas beforehand, then cool them and store in a box. If pre-fried, when ready to serve, wrap each paratha in parchment paper and then again in foil and reheat in a medium oven for 15 minutes.

Gajjar Ka Halwa
Carrot halwa V

I associate this dessert with winter. When I was growing up in India, we ate seasonally. The arrival of the red carrots in winter was always the food highlight for my family, as my father loved Gajjar Ka Halwa. With fruits and vegetables being flown in from abroad and the increased use of cold storage all year round, eating with the seasons is no longer the norm in Indian cities and larger towns. This recipe does require time, but serious elbow grease is required only when making the halwa in huge quantities. This is a dish for which you need to have great patience and a killer playlist in the background; this is not a quick dessert!

Serves 4–6

900 ml/1½ pints/3½ cups whole milk

500 g/1 lb 2 oz carrots, peeled and coarsely grated

3 small green cardamom pods

1 Indian bay leaf

50 g/1¾ oz/3½ tbsp ghee or unsalted butter

200 g/7 oz/1 cup granulated sugar

A handful of almond or pistachio slivers, to garnish (optional)

Double (heavy) cream or clotted cream

In a large pan, bring the milk to the boil. Add the grated carrots to the pan and bring the milk back to the boil.

Add the cardamom pods and bay leaf to the pan. Lower the heat to prevent the milk from burning, continue to simmer the milk while stirring at regular intervals to prevent it from catching on the base of the pan.

After approximately 2 hours, when all the milk has been absorbed, add the ghee or butter and the sugar. Continue to stir for a further 20 minutes until the sugar has dissolved and the carrot paste is moist but with no excess liquid left in the pan.

Serve the carrot halwa while still warm. I prefer to bring a large serving bowl to the table and encourage everyone to help themselves, taking as little or as much as their personal sweet tooth dictates! Alongside the halwa, serve bowls of almond or pistachio slivers, to scatter over the halwa, and thick cream, to dollop on the side.

Sooji Halwa Ladoo
Semolina halwa balls v

Indian desserts can often be too rich and sweet for many people. This is an ideal end to a festive meal as it is light and – unlike many other Indian desserts – it is soaked in neither cream nor milk. Another attraction of this dessert is that it takes 25–30 minutes to prepare and is not labour intensive, leaving you with more time to enjoy the party. 'Ladoo' is a generic name for any dessert, which is rolled into individual balls but, if you prefer, the halwa can be served warm in a bowl rather than rolled. Do grate the nutmeg yourself from the whole spice, as shop-bought ground nutmeg is a shadow of the whole spice.

Serves 6–8

¼ tsp good-quality saffron strands

1 piece cassia bark, 2.5 cm/1 inch long (see page 13)

2 whole cloves

150 g/5½ oz/¾ cup granulated sugar

125 ml/4 fl oz/½ cup melted ghee or unsalted butter

25 g/1 oz raisins (golden or green)

200 g/7 oz/1¼ cup fine semolina flour

½ tsp freshly grated nutmeg

½ tsp freshly crushed cardamom seeds

40 g/1½ oz cashew nuts, chopped

A few edible rose petals, to garnish (optional)

In a bowl, infuse the saffron strands in ½ tsp of tepid water. Set aside.

Place the cassia bark and cloves in a pan and cover with 500 ml/ 17 fl oz/2 cups cold water. Bring to a boil over a medium–high heat. Lower the heat, add the sugar to the pan and cook, stirring, until all the sugar crystals have dissolved.

In a large non-stick karai, wok or frying pan, heat the melted ghee or butter over a low–medium heat. Add the raisins and stir, then remove them with a slotted spoon just before they expand and burst. Add the raisins to the pan with the sugar syrup.

Now add the semolina flour to the pan with the ghee or butter, together with the grated nutmeg and crushed cardamom seeds. Gently stir until the grains of the semolina darken and smell toasted (approximately 10 minutes). Keep the heat low as you do not want to burn the semolina grains. Remove the pan from the heat and slowly add the sugar syrup, stirring constantly. The contents will sputter initially but then calm down.

Put the pan back on the heat and stir to break up any lumps. Keep the pan on the heat until all the sugar syrup has been absorbed. Towards the end of the cooking, add the chopped cashew nuts and the saffron-infused liquid.

Once the halwa is cool enough to handle, roll it into ladoos, or balls. Alternatively, you can serve the halwa as it is, warmed and placed in a serving bowl, and let your guests serve themselves.

To serve, scatter over a few edible rose petals to add a festive flourish to this dish.

Menu Suggestions

Within Ayurveda there are six basic principles of taste: sweet, sour, salty, bitter, pungent and astringent. Not every meal needs to include all these tastes, but it helps to know these principles in order to understand how many Indians eat with family and friends.

Contrasting textures, colours and flavours are usually how menu selections are made. In Bengal, a fish dish like Macher Jhol would never be served with a paratha; instead it would always be served with rice. Conversely, Bihari Kabab would not be served with rice. Some of these rice and bread traditions emerged simply because a region was a rice-growing area that grew no wheat, and vice versa, rather than because roti or rice was considered as incompatible with a dish. You do not need to follow these cultural rules or traditions when devising a menu for a party, but feel free to pair those dishes that most appeal to you.

You can follow the menu plans that I have suggested here, or you can pluck out the dishes that you most like the sound of to create your own feast. I have not added desserts to any of the menu suggestions; I will leave you to decide whether or not you want to add a dessert to your meal plan. As there are many easy-to-follow recipes online, I have not given a recipe for plain white basmati rice in this book, but a useful tip is to cook 75 g/2½ oz uncooked rice per person.

Feast for one
With leftovers for the next day.
Rogni Roti (page 53)
Masala Omelette (page 42)
Tengri Kabab (page 26)

Vegetarian menu for two
Tehri (page 25)
Courgette Sabzi (page 22)
Karai Paneer (page 31)
Zeera Aloo (page 21)

Vegan menu for two
Replace any ghee or unsalted butter in the recipes with vegetable oil.
Sukhi Bhindi (page 47)
Masoor Dal (page 39)
Tamatar Bharta (page 40)
Baingan Aloo (page 41)
Basmati rice

Pescetarian feast for two
Macher Malaikari (page 48)
Phali Ki Sabzi (page 51)
Chingri Bhaaja (page 28)
Basmati rice

Meat feast for two
Rogni Roti (page 53)
Chicken Bharta (page 46)
Palak Gosht (page 45)
Hari Phoolgobi Eggs (page 35)

Vegetarian/vegan family feast

Replace any ghee or unsalted butter in the recipes with vegetable oil.

Peela Pulao (page 64)

Begun Bhaja (page 73)

Mattar Paneer (page 85)

Channa Masala (page 84)

Bihari Saag (page 91)

Kari Patta Ka Kaddu (page 78)

Family feast

Keema Sua Pulao (page 69)

Paneer Malai Korma (page 74)

Murgh Rezala (page 66)

Shahi Kofta (page 77)

Dahi Baingan (page 72)

Family feast to impress

Mattar Pulao (page 79)

Shorshe Maach (page 90)

Dum Gosht (page 94)

Hyderabadi Tamatar Ka Cutt (page 80)

Chukander Raita (page 70)

Baingan Bharta (page 83)

Vegetarian feasting with friends

Khichree (page 121)

Gobi Musallam (page 122)

Aloo Dum (page 104)

Tomato Raita (page 111)

Vegan feasting with friends

Anglo-Indian Coconut Rice (page 106)

Kaju Aloo (page 113)

Bharwa Simla Mirch + Aloo Dum (page 113)

Channa Dal (page 110)

Feasting with friends

Machi Kabab (page 120)

Zafran Murgh Korma (page 102)

Anglo-Indian Ball Curry (page 108)

Puri (page 114) or Sheermal (page 117)

Pescetarian celebratory feast

A good menu when you are cooking under time pressure.

Dum Ki Machli (page 154)

Lachedar Paratha (page 167)

Kali Dal (page 158)

Tamatar Ki Chutney (page 160)

Kachumber (page 166)

No-expense-spared celebratory feast

Raan (page 144)

Macher Jhol (page 156)

Navratan Pulao (page 162)

Narangi Korma (page 152)

Kachumber (page 166)

Rajma (page 159)

Index

Acknowledgements

I dedicate this book to my mother, Faizana, the person who taught me how to cook. She is also the inspiration behind Darjeeling Express and this cookbook.

To my father Farrukh, my husband Mushtaq, my children Ariz and Fariz, and my siblings Amna and Arif, you have all been the wind beneath my wings. To my hugely supportive and loving mother-in-law, Saeeda, and to my cousin, Sadia, I am so grateful for your love and support. I would also like to thank Asha, Maham, Shefaly, Tarunima, Wincie and Farah Kadir.

There are two women who I especially want to thank, both of whom exerted a huge influence on my life. The first is my 'ayah' ma who came into my family to help look after my mother when she was born, but stayed on for decades and helped to raise me and my siblings. She cooked simple dishes using very few ingredients. I learnt from her that less is often more when cooking, but that the most important ingredient in any dish is love.

The second is my aunt Bibi who visited me often in Cambridge and, on her first trip to my home, spent the first evening apologizing to my husband when she realized that I could not cook. In my Cambridge kitchen, she taught me how to make my first few dishes and gifted to me a proper cooking pot. Sadly, Bibi never got to taste my food as she passed away before I had the chance to cook properly for her.

I met my literary agent, Rachel Conway, by chance a couple of years ago, while serving her at a pop-up restaurant I was running in London. After service ended, I sat down to chat to Rachel as she seemed so interested in the origin of the dishes served during the course of that evening. The conversations continued over a few more meals, which eventually led to this book. Thank you, Rachel, for believing in me.

The creative forces of Kim Lightbody, Valerie Berry and Tabitha Hawkins have produced the wonderful food photography captured in these pages. I love the evocative colours of the images and the simplicity of styling.

A special mention for my friend Ming Tang-Evans, who journeyed with me to Calcutta and shot all the photographs taken on location in India that you see within the pages of this book. Ming has taken photographs of my food for years; I love the way he captures the soul of India through his lens.

Thanks also to the illustrator Alan Berry Rhys.

Last but not least, I would like to thank the awesome commissioning team at Pavilion Books, Stephanie Milner and Katie Cowan. Writing this cookbook and setting up my restaurant happened at exactly the same time, so I was concerned at just how traumatic that might be. But Stephanie and Katie, along with the creativity of Laura Russell and Helen Lewis, were all hugely supportive and understanding. Despite some tight deadlines, I have never felt harried. Finally, a big thank you to Lisa Pendreigh for doing such a brilliant job in editing my words and recipes, for picking up not just my English typos but also all my incorrect Hindi spellings!

I really enjoyed writing this book because I have been given the opportunity to share my stories and recipes, and was allowed the space to write. Thank you Pavilion for breathing life into my vision and producing this book of which I am so proud.

Photography pages 2, 16–17, 23, 24, 27, 29, 37, 38, 43, 44, 49, 50, 52, 59, 60–61, 67, 68, 71, 75, 76, 81, 82, 93, 97, 98–99, 103, 105, 107, 112, 115, 116, 123, 124, 127, 129, 132–133, 137, 140, 145, 149, 155, 157, 161, 168, 171 and 172 by Kim Lightbody

Photography end papers and pages 4, 5, 8, 12, 15, 18, 19, 33, 54, 55, 62, 87, 88, 100, 118, 135, 150, 151, 165, 181 and 184 by Ming Tang-Evans

Cover illustration by Alan Berry Rhys featuring photograph by Ming Tang-Evans